THE 20 LAWS THAT GOVERN
THE FINANCIAL ANOINTING

ALSO FROM REVIVAL TODAY

Financial Overflow

Dominion Over Sickness and Disease

Boldly I Come

Twenty Secrets for an Unbreakable Marriage

How to Dominate in a Wicked Nation

Seven Wrong Relationships

Everything a Man Should Be

Understanding the World in Light of Bible Prophecy

Are You Going Through a Crisis?

The 20 Laws that Govern the Financial Anointing

Books are available in EBOOK and PAPERBACK through your favorite online book retailer or by request from your local bookstore.

THE 20 LAWS THAT GOVERN
THE FINANCIAL ANOINTING

JONATHAN SHUTTLESWORTH

Foreword by
JESSE DUPLANTIS

Without limiting the rights under copyright(s) reserved below, no part of this publication may be reproduced, stored in or introduced into a retrieval system, or transmitted, in any form, or by any means (electronic, mechanical, photocopying, recording, or otherwise) without the prior permission of the publisher and the copyright owner.

The content of this book is provided "AS IS." The Publisher and the Author make no guarantees or warranties as to the accuracy, adequacy or completeness of or results to be obtained from using the content of this book, including any information that can be accessed through hyperlinks or otherwise, and expressly disclaim any warranty expressed or implied, including but not limited to implied warranties of merchantability or fitness for a particular purpose. This limitation of liability shall apply to any claim or cause whatsoever, whether such claim or cause arises in contract, tort, or otherwise. In short, you, the reader, are responsible for your choices and the results they bring.

The scanning, uploading, and distributing of this book via the internet or via any other means without the permission of the publisher and copyright owner is illegal and punishable by law. Please purchase only authorized copies, and do not participate in or encourage piracy of copyrighted materials. Your support of the author's rights is appreciated.

Copyright © 2023 by Revival Today. All rights reserved.

Unless otherwise indicated, all Scripture quotations are taken from the Holy Bible, New Living Translation, copyright © 1996, 2004, 2015 by Tyndale House Foundation. Used by permission of Tyndale House Publishers, a Division of Tyndall House Ministries, Carol Stream, Illinois 60188. All rights reserved.

Scriptures marked KJV are taken from the KING JAMES VERSION (KJV): KING JAMES VERSION, public domain.

Scriptures marked NKJV are taken from the NEW KING JAMES VERSION (NKJV): Scripture taken from the NEW KING JAMES VERSION®. Copyright© 1982 by Thomas Nelson, Inc. Used by permission. All rights reserved.

Scripture text within the body, shown in italics, is from multiple unspecified translations or the author's paraphrase.

Book design by eBook Prep
www.ebookprep.com

September 2023
ISBN: 978-1-64457-336-5 Paperback
ISBN: 978-1-64457-648-8 Hardcover

Rise UP Publications
644 Shrewsbury Commons Ave
Ste 249
Shrewsbury PA 17361
United States of America

www.riseUPpublications.com
Phone: 866-846-5123

CONTENTS

Foreword   11
Introduction   15

Law One   19
The Law of Positive Outlook

Law Two   23
The Elisha Law: Looking to Pay

Law Three   29
The Law of Contentment

Law Four   35
The Law of Proper Value

Law Five   39
The Law of Servanthood

Law Six   49
The Law of Solution

Law Seven   55
The Law of Association

Law Eight   63
The Law of Covenant Land Ownership

Law Nine   81
The Law of The Family

Law Ten   103
The Law of Joy

Law Eleven   109
The Law of Protection

Law Twelve   123
The Law of Debt Refusal

Law Thirteen   135
The Law of Holiness

Law Fourteen   141
The Law of Love and Honor

Law Fifteen   153
The Law of Significant Seed Sowing

Law Sixteen   169
The Law of Diligence

Law Seventeen   191
The Law of Confession

Law Eighteen   211
The Law of Thanksgiving and Praise

Law Nineteen   223
The Millionaire Law

Law Twenty   239
The Law of Continual Victory and Increase

Afterword   253
Author Photo   256
About the Author   258

"If someone does not care about money, they do not care about people, their own life, their family, or their own dreams and accomplishments, and they have little or no regard for the Gospel of Jesus Christ."

— JONATHAN SHUTTLESWORTH

FOREWORD

BY DR. JESSE DUPLANTIS

What you're holding in your hands right now has the power of God to change not only your life, but also how you function in this world. And so it is my great honor to write and recommend Jonathan Shuttlesworth and this book, The 20 Laws That Govern the Financial Anointing, to you. It is not only revolutionary; it is revelationary! For those of you who are reading this and already know about Jonathan and his ministry, then this comes as no surprise to you and you're ready to dive in. But for those of you who are just learning of Jonathan and reading his material for the first time, all I can say is, get ready to be blessed!

Now, I know something about the financial anointing because it is on my life greatly. I do not mean that in a prideful way—it's just what the Lord has done in my life, and I make no apologies for the blessings of God or what He's done for me. I just do what God says in His Word, and He alone gets all the praise and glory! And as you read this book, you will discover, as Jonathan so passionately makes clear, that this financial anointing belongs to you, too, as a born-again child

FOREWORD

of God. But the key is that you have to be a doer of the Word and not just a hearer only.

What I love about Jonathan is his straightforwardness and his unapologetic stand for the Bible and everything it says, and, yes, that includes finances. I really enjoyed this book and the uniqueness of Jonathan's writing. I was drawn to a couple of statements he made in The Law of Proper Value that are so important for people to understand. Jonathan says, "...people put a premium on going through hardship...But you only have to go through the school of hard knocks if you bypass the school of wisdom." That's so true. The Bible tells us in Proverbs 4:7 that wisdom is the principal thing, and that if you get wisdom, you will get understanding. And let me tell you, Jonathan Shuttleworth has it! He goes on to say, "God doesn't teach through pain. God doesn't teach through hardship. God doesn't teach through failure. God teaches by His Word." I just love that. God is a good God and a good Father—He's not an abuser. He's looking to help us and bless us, not to hurt us. He doesn't set us up for failure. He's designed us and positioned us for greatness and victory.

Every law taught in this book will minister greatly to you, just as they did me. There are so many things I could write about and share with you, it would take me 40 pages alone just in this foreword! But the bottom line is this: You need to read this book, and then read it again. Get it inside your spirit, and then let it go through your soul to a crucified body and you'll be so blessed, it'll change your way of thinking. This book will give you motivation for accumulation and revelation which has no limitation!

You should read this book slowly and take time to digest it, because it's not what you eat in the Word but what you digest in the Word that matters—it will give you exactly what you need to grow and succeed in life. This book will help you to understand life the way God designed it and the way it should be lived. You see, it's not just about our experiences in life that make it good; it's about the Word of the living God on the inside of us and working in our everyday life that makes this life extraordinary. Experience doesn't make you a believer. The Word of God makes you a believer.

The financial laws Jonathan talks about are straight from the Word, and they are important for you to know and understand to live the life God wants for you—not because you're good or you earned it, but because He's good and you're His child! As you study this book along with the Word and determine to live this way, you will discover for yourself that God will indeed give you a positive outlook. He will give you continual increase. He will give you solutions. He will give you association. He will give you contentment and joy. God wants all these things for you, and so much more! That's what this book is all about.

Again, I encourage you to read this slowly and meditate and concentrate on what this man is saying to you because he's talking to you through the Spirit of God. It will challenge you. It will change you. It will honor God. It will honor Jonathan's ministry. But it will also show you just how important you are to God as a believer. So, receive it today. And if there's one thing I could impart to you, it would be this: Don't put things off into the future. Receive it in the now because faith was made for the now!

So, enjoy yourself as you read and study this book. You're about ready to grow in the Spirit of God.

Dr. Jesse Duplantis
Evangelist, Author, TV Host;
President and Founder of Jesse Duplantis Ministries

INTRODUCTION

UNDERSTANDING THE FINANCIAL ANOINTING

Helping the poor begins with a decision to not be one of them. You can't help people if *you* need help. How would you follow Jesus's basic command to feed the hungry if you don't have enough food? How would you follow Jesus's basic command to clothe the naked if you're struggling to buy school clothes for your own children? If you want to help the poor, start by deciding not to be poor yourself.

> Now Elijah, who was from Tishbe in Gilead, told King Ahab, "As surely as the Lord, the God of Israel, lives—the God I serve—there will be no dew or rain during the next few years until I give the word!"
> Then the Lord said to Elijah, "Go to the east and hide by Kerith Brook, near where it enters the Jordan River. Drink from the brook and eat what the ravens bring you, for I have commanded them to bring you food."
> So Elijah did as the Lord told him and camped beside

INTRODUCTION

Kerith Brook, east of the Jordan. The ravens brought him bread and meat each morning and evening, and he drank from the brook. But after a while the brook dried up, for there was no rainfall anywhere in the land.

Then the Lord said to Elijah, "Go and live in the village of Zarephath, near the city of Sidon. I have instructed a widow there to feed you."

So he went to Zarephath. As he arrived at the gates of the village, he saw a widow gathering sticks, and he asked her, "Would you please bring me a little water in a cup?" As she was going to get it, he called to her, "Bring me a bite of bread, too."

But she said, "I swear by the Lord your God that I don't have a single piece of bread in the house. And I have only a handful of flour left in the jar and a little cooking oil in the bottom of the jug. I was just gathering a few sticks to cook this last meal, and then my son and I will die."

But Elijah said to her, "Don't be afraid! Go ahead and do just what you've said, but make a little bread for me first. Then use what's left to prepare a meal for yourself and your son. For this is what the Lord, the God of Israel, says: There will always be flour and olive oil left in your containers until the time when the Lord sends rain and the crops grow again!"

So she did as Elijah said, and she and Elijah and her family continued to eat for many days.

INTRODUCTION

> There was always enough flour and olive oil left in the containers, just as the Lord had promised through Elijah.
>
> — 1 KINGS 17:1-16

It is impossible to read this passage of scripture—and it's one of many—without concluding that there is a supernatural financial anointing. Just as some people operate in a healing anointing or an anointing for prophecy, there is another anointing that very few people talk about, and even fewer people operate in. I've called it the financial anointing. Those who have it don't need to do fundraising; they don't have to try to generate capital.

There's something you can carry upon your life by the Holy Ghost that draws wealth to you. Elijah wasn't trying to find food; food was finding Elijah. When Elijah went to a home where a lady had nothing to eat, she went from not having enough to never running out—without ever starting a GoFundMe, and without announcing anything on Facebook. That is a financial anointing. Most people don't have it, and getting a loan doesn't produce it.

> Thou preparest a table before me in the presence of mine enemies: thou anointest my head with oil; my cup runneth over.
>
> — PSALM 23:5 (KJV)

Without money—without finances—you can't do what God's called you to do. Life becomes a frustration. But on the flip side, when you have an abundance of money, you can dream big dreams and accomplish big tasks. If you took a minister who had 10 times the

INTRODUCTION

financial anointing as another minister, but he had 1/10th of the finances, the minister with one 1/10th of the anointing and a hundred times more finances will be able to accomplish more for the kingdom of God. Think about it; if you take the most powerful preacher you know, but he only has enough money to put a crusade together with a hundred people in attendance, and then take another guy who is not nearly as good of a preacher but has the finances to put on a proper crusade with 20,000 people in the crowd, he'll far out-produce the man with the crusade with a hundred people. Even if he only gets a fraction of those in attendance saved.

Money matters. If you don't care about money, you don't care about people. If you don't care about money, you don't care about your own life. If you don't care about money, you don't care about your family. If you don't care about money, you don't care about your own dreams and accomplishing the things God has given you to do. If you care about those things, you want to understand the laws that govern the financial anointing. You can see through the life of Elijah and the life of Jesus that there is a financial anointing. There is a supernatural anointing that affects money and provision. Just as laws govern science, thermodynamics, and health, there are laws governing the financial anointing. We're going to explore 20 of them together.

LAW ONE

THE LAW OF POSITIVE OUTLOOK

You will never prosper without The Law of Positive Outlook that affects every area of your life and your future. You will meet people who struggle financially, and the vast majority of the time, they're very negative people. It's like a two-pronged attack of the Devil; he has you go through hard times, so you forfeit your joy and positive outlook and exchange it for a negative outlook. Many were raised in homes where their parents verbally instilled a negative outlook on life, perhaps due to financial struggles. They might have said things like, "You'll see when you get older," or, "It must be nice playing all the time. Wait till you're my age, and you have to work for a living." Their words conveyed that life is riddled with hardship, bills, and expenses. You'll never be prosperous if you receive that mentality into your spirit. Joseph never forfeited his positive outlook as a slave or as a prisoner; he received a dream from God that one day he would rule. Even though all outward circumstances contradicted what God had told him, he held to that dream. He honored the law of positive outlook, and in the end, he didn't die a prisoner. He didn't die a slave. Instead, he died as prime minister of the most powerful nation in the world.

The person who thinks the world will end in the next three months will not build anything or invest in anything and probably won't grow. Those who focus their belief on the dollar collapsing and who fear an ensuing apocalypse will be paralyzed. The first instruction Elijah gave the widow (after she voiced her concerns) was, "Don't be afraid." Fear paralyzes. Those who study what happens behind closed doors, including the manipulation of markets, the corruption of governments, election interference, and tampering, they understand that the findings of their studies and research hold true, but their knowledge has paralyzed them. In that state of fear, it is difficult to study Bible prophecy and "end time" events. This results in a lack of productivity.

This present world will end, but there are two things to note. First, Jesus said: *Before that day there will be buying and selling, farming and building. People will be married and being given in marriage.* The New Living Translation adds: *It will be business as usual before I return.* Many will be surprised that there is not a pre-apocalypse to the apocalypse. People will be buying and selling, which means the economy will be functional before the return of Christ. Second, despite several "Bible prophecies" predicting catastrophic events happening toward the end of time, none of this nullifies the command the Lord gave to the believer to occupy until His return. His instruction remains to *be fruitful and multiply.* God didn't just make productivity available; God commanded productivity and multiplication. An unproductive person is living in rebellion against God's first command.

Focusing on the negative prevents people from operating in the financial anointing. The believer should instead focus on the promises of God. These promises do not change based on a newly elected president. They don't change based on corruption or schemes plotted behind closed doors. When God has blessed someone, no other person or thing can curse them. Do you see a dim future for yourself or a bright future?

The Word of God declares the following in Jeremiah…

> "For I know the plans I have for you," says the Lord.
> "They are plans for good and not for disaster, to
> give you a future and a hope."
>
> — JEREMIAH 29:11

It's impossible to focus on what God says about you and your life and simultaneously have a negative outlook. God's Word is not subject to the decisions of the International Monetary Fund, the World Economic Forum, or the United Nations. No group can plot to destroy one's future because it's not in the Devil's hands; it's in God's hands.

I'm sure the readers of this book have endured difficult circumstances. I'm sure there are things you wish would have turned out differently. Don't give the Devil a second victory by allowing that negative experience to turn you into a negative person. Instead, maintain your joy in the Lord, and maintain a heartfelt belief that your future is bright because it's in the hands of God. If you maintain that belief, you've laid the foundation to walk in the financial anointing.

LAW TWO

THE ELISHA LAW: LOOKING TO PAY

I'm not in need; God sent me to my generation to lift the financial needs off of people, not to burden them. I have more than enough; my head is anointed, and my cup overflows. This is The Elisha Law: Looking to Pay.

> One day the widow of a member of the group of prophets came to Elisha and cried out, "My husband who served you is dead, and you know how he feared the Lord. But now a creditor has come, threatening to take my two sons as slaves."
> "What can I do to help you?" Elisha asked. "Tell me, what do you have in the house?"
> "Nothing at all, except a flask of olive oil," she replied.
> And Elisha said, "Borrow as many empty jars as you can from your friends and neighbors. Then go into your house with your sons and shut the door behind you. Pour olive oil from your flask into the jars, setting each one aside when it is filled."

> So she did as she was told. Her sons kept bringing jars to her, and she filled one after another. Soon every container was full to the brim!
> "Bring me another jar," she said to one of her sons.
> "There aren't any more!" he told her. And then the olive oil stopped flowing.
> When she told the man of God what had happened, he said to her, "Now sell the olive oil and pay your debts, and you and your sons can live on what is left over."
>
> — 2 KINGS 4:1-7

When the widow told Elisha about her problem, he didn't say, "Well, join the club. I have my own financial problems. We're all struggling." Instead, Elisha realized he carried an anointing to lift people out of poverty. I was going to call this second law, "look to pay," but that's not catchy. Now that I titled it something else, I want you to catch that and not forget it; looking to pay. What do I mean by that? Look at the story of the feeding of the 5,000.

> After this, Jesus crossed over to the far side of the Sea of Galilee, also known as the Sea of Tiberias. A huge crowd kept following him wherever he went, because they saw his miraculous signs as he healed the sick. Then Jesus climbed a hill and sat down with his disciples around him. (It was nearly time for the Jewish Passover celebration.) Jesus soon saw a huge crowd of people coming to look for him. Turning to Philip, he asked, "Where can we buy bread to feed all these people?" He was testing

> Philip, for he already knew what he was going to do.
> Philip replied, "Even if we worked for months, we wouldn't have enough money to feed them!"
> Then Andrew, Simon Peter's brother, spoke up. "There's a young boy here with five barley loaves and two fish. But what good is that with this huge crowd?"
> "Tell everyone to sit down," Jesus said. So, they all sat down on the grassy slopes. (The men alone numbered about 5,000.) Then Jesus took the loaves, gave thanks to God, and distributed them to the people. Afterward he did the same with the fish. And they all ate as much as they wanted. After everyone was full, Jesus told his disciples, "Now gather the leftovers, so that nothing is wasted." So they picked up the pieces and filled twelve baskets with scraps left by the people who had eaten from the five barley loaves.
>
> — JOHN 6:1-13

This is another instance of the financial anointing in the Bible, along with the story of Elisha by prophetic instruction, multiplying the widow's oil. There is a financial anointing for both instances mentioned above; the only way it could have happened was supernatural.

Look to pay. I had never seen a guest minister pay for a meal in my entire life; it's not how things were done. If you were a minister, a well-to-do family from the church took you out to eat. They're always treated. They're the guest. When I was a child, we went to eat at the

Red Lobster with my grandfather, who was a minister, and a large group of other ministers with their families. There were probably over 30 people, and everyone ordered crab legs. The bill had to be enormous, and I was waiting for the server to split the checks. Instead, my grandfather told the server, "Have everybody's bill brought to me." Then he paid the entire bill! That made such an impression on me when I was 13 years old that I'm still talking about it at 41. I had never seen somebody pay—let alone a minister—for so many families' bills. When I saw that, I liked it. Most people are looking for somebody to pay for them; they think being blessed is someone buying your meal, but true blessing doesn't celebrate what it receives. True blessing celebrates what it gives.

Jesus followed the Elisha law. Provision comes from me. I don't need provision, I create provision. Since receiving that revelation out of Jesus feeding the 5,000, I've tried to feed as many people as I can on a regular basis. When I eat at a restaurant, I often ask the waitress to bring me two or three other people's bills. Sometimes, I'll pay for everybody in the restaurant. I'm not saying you have to do that, but it's pretty hard to read the story of Jesus feeding the 5,000, then go out to eat with four other people and ask to split the check. When was the last time you paid for a meal for someone outside of your own family?

The Elisha law, put very simply, is believing in the depth of your heart that you are not in need, but that God has sent you to your generation to erase needs; you are looking to pay. When you make that mentality switch, the financial anointing is drawn to you because the financial anointing does not primarily work to meet your needs. The financial anointing works through you, the financial anointing deals with overflow—more than your cup can hold. Until you have eyes toward other people—to help others outside of your cup—your cup will never overflow. You could never get me to say, "I have a need," with a gun to my head. I can't say it.

> The Lord is my shepherd; I have all that I need.
>
> — PSALM 23:1

Paul, summing up his ministry, said…

> Not that I was ever in need, for I have learned how to be content with whatever I have.
>
> — PHILIPPIANS 4:11

Well, that's a stark contrast to how most Christians and ministers speak, saying, "We have a need." They are always playing from behind financially. That is not scriptural. Deuteronomy 28 says: *I will fill your storehouses with grain.* Storehouses filled with grain imply that needs are met, and there is an abundance in reserve. If your storehouse is full, you don't need to borrow. That's why the same passage in Deuteronomy says *you will lend only, thou shalt not borrow.* To our debt-obsessed culture, that sounds impossible. But I have a question; if you're never in need because the Lord is your shepherd and you don't lack, how could you ever need to borrow? Borrowing implies a need, and the Bible says that *God supplies all your needs.* Although we've been trained to think it's normal to be in need, scripturally, it's abnormal. Not only am I not in debt, but if I see a widow in severe debt, God has empowered me to get her out of debt. If a multitude has a food deficit, God has empowered me to erase their food deficit. I'm not in need; I meet needs. That's the Elisha law, looking to pay, not looking for somebody to pay for you.

LAW THREE

THE LAW OF CONTENTMENT

M oney can't master you; you have to master money. And one of the secrets is The Law of Contentment.

> Yet true godliness with contentment is itself great wealth. After all, we brought nothing with us when we came into the world, and we can't take anything with us when we leave it. So if we have enough food and clothing, let us be content.
> But people who long to be rich fall into temptation and are trapped by many foolish and harmful desires that plunge them into ruin and destruction. For the love of money is the root of all kinds of evil. And some people, craving money, have wandered from the true faith and pierced themselves with many sorrows.
>
> — 1 TIMOTHY 6:6-10

People who don't believe in prosperity think people like me are unaware of Bible verses like this. I was preaching in Vermont once, and I spoke on the blessing of Abraham. A young man who had been to Bible college walked up to me afterward with his Bible open and an angry look in his eyes, waiting to speak to me. Then when it was his turn in line, I said, "Can I help you?" He said, "Well, you preached tonight that God wants people to have money. I want to read something to you." And he read the above passage. He said, "What do you have to say about that?" I said, "Does the chapter end where you stopped?" He said, "No." I said, "Read the rest to me." And this is what it says.

> But you, Timothy, are a man of God; so run from all these evil things. Pursue righteousness and a godly life, along with faith, love, perseverance, and gentleness. Fight the good fight for the true faith. Hold tightly to the eternal life to which God has called you, which you have declared so well before many witnesses. And I charge you before God, who gives life to all, and before Christ Jesus, who gave a good testimony before Pontius Pilate, that you obey this command without wavering. Then no one can find fault with you from now until our Lord Jesus Christ comes again.
>
> — 1 TIMOTHY 6:11-14

> Teach those who are rich in this world not to be proud and not to trust in their money, which is so unreliable. Their trust should be in God, who richly gives us all we need for our enjoyment. Tell them to use their money to do good. They should be rich

> in good works and generous to those in need, always being ready to share with others. By doing this they will be storing up their treasure as a good foundation for the future so that they may experience true life.
>
> — 1 TIMOTHY 6:17-19

The young man responded, "Oh, it helps if you read the whole thing."

God spoke to my overseer in the ministry, Rodney Howard-Browne, and told him, "When everything means nothing to you, I'll give you everything." When God speaks to you about giving, often, He's testing you to make sure that money and possessions only have a place in your hand, not in your heart... that clothes are only something you wear, not something you love. When the Holy Spirit speaks to you to give away something of value, it's a test to see if you're qualified to handle true riches.

Money in-the-hand is a tool. Money in-the-heart is a poison. If you love money, watches, clothes, shoes, and a certain kind of vehicle, it greatly hinders you from operating in the financial anointing. Paul said that people who allow themselves to love "things" have pierced themselves with many sorrows and destroyed themselves. When you love a material thing, a house, or a possession, it opens the door to temptation. The temptation might be to steal, be dishonest in business practices, or get rich quick to obtain material assets. But when you are content with what you have, you can give properly, closing the door to greed, unethical business practices, and theft.

"When everything means nothing to you, I'll give you everything." When material possessions have no hold on you, God will flood you with them. God enjoys blessing His children, but He does not enjoy giving them material wealth and possessions that destroy them or take His place.

I have a very nice watch; it means a lot to me because of the person who gave it to me. If the Lord spoke to me to give it away right now, it would be off my wrist in under 20 seconds. If the Lord asked me to, there's nothing I own that I'd think twice about giving.

Many years ago, during our "21 Days of Prayer and Fasting," a man came to me saying, "I have a classic car that's worth a lot of money. When I was praying at the altar, the Lord told me to give it to you for your ministry." I knew right then that he wasn't going to give it. The Lord has never told me to tell someone that I will give them something. He tells me to just give it. When people start telling you that the Lord spoke to them to give, they're already wrestling, and usually, they're wrestling a losing match. So, I said, "Praise the Lord."

He called me about six weeks later and said, "Jonathan, I talked it over with some of the men in a Bible study, and they said it's not really wise to give the car away, and God doesn't expect it of me." It's odd to me that people have the Lord tell them something, then they run it by a person or group of people and allow those people to veto what the Holy Spirit said. He said, "I know I shook your hand and gave you my word, and my word is my bond. So, if you still want me to give it to you, I'll honor my word." When he said that, the Scripture came up in my spirit of what Peter said to Ananias and Sapphira, "The money was yours to give or not to give." So, I said, "No, the car is yours to give."

I'm not going to have somebody give something to me because I told them, "Well, you gave me your word." The money is his to give or not to give, and the car is his to give or not to give. If a person wants to disobey God, that's their business. He responded with, "Okay," and

I've never heard from him again. I've never seen him after that. Obviously, it would convict him to see me again because it would be a reminder of his rebellion. I don't know why he would keep the car anyway. Every time he sees it in the garage, it will be a glowing reminder of his disobedience. He'll never be able to ride in that car again and enjoy himself. When the Lord told me to give that SUV, if I'd kept it, I would have never had a pleasurable ride in it for the rest of my life because of violating the law of contentment.

I'm increasing because God commanded me to increase, and God's anointed me to increase, but I'm not striving to increase. When he anoints your head with oil, your cup just runs over. You don't have to try to get it to run over.

I've never messaged someone privately, asking them if I could please have some money. I'm not *trying* to get it—money follows me. Whatever I don't have, I'm content. There's nothing I possess that I actually care about.

If you don't observe the law of contentment, you'll be owned by materialism. You'll never be able to build a big enough house. You cannot master something that controls you. So, if wealth and possessions control you, you can't operate in the anointing. The anointing is dominion, and you can't have dominion over something that has dominion over you.

LAW FOUR

THE LAW OF PROPER VALUE

Life can be hard, but it will be really hard without wisdom. This is The Law of Proper Value. But the longer title is The Law of Placing the Proper Value on Wisdom.

> Wisdom shouts in the streets. She cries out in the public square. She calls to the crowds along the main street, to those gathered in front of the city gate:
>
> "How long, you simpletons, will you insist on being simpleminded? How long will you mockers relish your mocking? How long will you fools hate knowledge? Come and listen to my counsel. I'll share my heart with you and make you wise.
>
> "I called you so often, but you wouldn't come. I reached out to you, but you paid no attention. You ignored my advice and rejected the correction I offered. So I will laugh when you are in trouble! I will mock you when disaster overtakes you—when

calamity overtakes you like a storm, when disaster engulfs you like a cyclone, and anguish and distress overwhelm you.

"When they cry for help, I will not answer. Though they anxiously search for me, they will not find me. For they hated knowledge and chose not to fear the LORD. They rejected my advice and paid no attention when I corrected them. Therefore, they must eat the bitter fruit of living their own way, choking on their own schemes. For simpletons turn away from me—to death. Fools are destroyed by their own complacency. But all who listen to me will live in peace, untroubled by fear of harm."

— PROVERBS 1:20-33

There was a struggling minister I knew of years ago. One day he complained, "I contacted a certain ministry that's a very well-known famous ministry and asked them if they could give me $10,000. And I never heard back from them. It would be very easy for them to give me $10,000, but they won't do it," he sneered.

He put a value on the money which that ministry had. He never read one of their books or teachings and had never been to one of their conferences. He put a high value on the money their wisdom produced and zero value on the wisdom that produced the overflow of money.

Bishop David Oyedepo probably has the largest, most financially prosperous ministry on Earth. Back when his church was small, and he was poor, the minister he worked for had a worldwide ministry. When Bishop Oyedepo was in this man's office, the man pointed at a duffel bag in the corner full of American money. He said, "Reach in that bag and take all you want for your wife, ministry, and yourself." That sounds like a dream come true, but Bishop David Oyedepo responded, "I don't want what's in the bag. I want what you know and what you have that created the money in the bag." The wisdom that produces the money never stops producing.

Sadly, if a church opens up a food pantry, or a clothing closet for people that need food and clothes, the parking lot's full of people. But, if they do a teaching session on finances, they'll be fortunate to have three people show up. And probably none of the people that show up for the teaching go to the food pantry. *Wisdom calls for a hearing in the street, but no one will listen. So, I'll laugh when you're in trouble and I'll mock you when you're having problems*—God wrote that.

I want to ask you a question: what books do you own and have read about finances? Financial increase? Investing? Revelation on money? Secondly, what events have you attended, hosted by people who have mastered money? From whom do you seek wisdom, so you're not wasting 40 years learning what they already know? And lastly, who are you consistently listening to that has mastered money, real estate, and investing? If you don't have a current voice on those subjects, those subjects will always remain a mystery to you. In your mind, rich people will always be people who are lucky or evil.

> Wisdom is the principal thing; therefore get wisdom:
> and with all thy getting get understanding.
>
> — PROVERBS 4:7 (KJV)

In our culture, people put a premium on going through hardship. People brag about hardship. But you only have to go through the school of hard knocks if you bypass the school of wisdom. Any lesson you learn in life can be learned ahead of time by the Word of God and by listening to people who have already gone through what you're going through. Life, marriage, finances, starting a business; there's vast wisdom readily available for anybody who wants to listen. If you bypass it, you bypass it to your own peril.

On the flip side, if you place a high premium on financial wisdom, you sow effortlessly and with ease. God doesn't teach through pain. God doesn't teach through hardship. God doesn't teach through failure. God teaches by his Word. According to Proverbs 1, God places a high premium on wisdom, and he has no respect for people who don't share the same high regard for wisdom.

When you read the Bible, there's a verse that says *be followers of them who by faith and patience have obtained the promises of God.* Not explained the promises of God...obtained the promises of God.

If you want to operate in the healing anointing, anybody can talk about their thoughts on healing, but you should follow those who have obtained the manifestation of that promise. Listen to people who have had blind eyes opened miraculously, deaf ears opened, and seen the cripple walk. Those are the people to listen to. On the subject of money, you can listen to any idiot talk about their thoughts on money, but if you listen to the people who have obtained the promise, who operate in overflow, who are the lender only and not the borrower, you're going to get wisdom from the heart of God that will transform your life.

LAW FIVE

THE LAW OF SERVANTHOOD

The Law of Servanthood is seeing yourself as a servant of Christ.

> "Again, the Kingdom of Heaven can be illustrated by the story of a man going on a long trip. He called together his servants and entrusted his money to them while he was gone. He gave five bags of silver to one, two bags of silver to another, and one bag of silver to the last—dividing it in proportion to their abilities. He then left on his trip.
> "The servant who received the five bags of silver began to invest the money and earned five more. The servant with two bags of silver also went to work and earned two more. But the servant who received the one bag of silver dug a hole in the ground and hid the master's money.
> "After a long time their master returned from his trip and called them to give an account of how they had

> used his money. The servant to whom he had entrusted the five bags of silver came forward with five more and said, 'Master, you gave me five bags of silver to invest, and I have earned five more.'
>
> "The master was full of praise. 'Well done, my good and faithful servant. You have been faithful in handling this small amount, so now I will give you many more responsibilities. Let's celebrate together!'
>
> "The servant who had received the two bags of silver came forward and said, 'Master, you gave me two bags of silver to invest, and I have earned two more.'
>
> "The master said, 'Well done, my good and faithful servant. You have been faithful in handling this small amount, so now I will give you many more responsibilities. Let's celebrate together!'"
>
> — MATTHEW 25:14-23

In Matthew 25, the man who went away on a long trip is about Jesus going to heaven and the time before he comes back. He entrusted money to his servants, and the servant who got commended understood what he had been entrusted with; he was expected to multiply.

You'll always be limited if you see yourself as a free agent. Many people see their life as separate from the kingdom of God. "This here is my thing, that there is God's thing. Good luck, God. All the best to you in advancing your agenda. Good luck building your kingdom. I have my thing. But I need your help! Help me get a house. Help me with everything I need." Such people have no concern for their master's work. They are like free agents who attend church, and once in a while, they chip off some money for God.

Some people have been serving the Lord for 25 years or more and still argue about tithing, giving God 10%. Then you have good servants who see everything they have as coming from God's hand and know they are expected to use it to produce for His kingdom; that person will prosper.

Of all these laws, this is the one law that has led me to prosperity. My life is not my own, and my money is not mine. The longer Paul went in his ministry, the farther he went down this trail. "I, Paul, an apostle of the Lord, Jesus Christ. I, Paul, a servant of the Lord, Jesus Christ. I, Paul, a slave of Christ Jesus." That was his mentality; I'll go where you want me to go, I'll do what you want me to do, and I'll say what you want me to say. Kingdom first, Kingdom everything. A God-first lifestyle.

When it comes to tithing, 10% of what I have does not belong to God, everything I have belongs to God, and he asked me to plant 10%; there's a reward attached to that. It's not my money.

I've been with ministers who felt the other guy was crooked when negotiating business for their church or ministry. They would say, "You realize this is not business money. This is not my money. This is God's money." And a chill would go up the spine of the person they were dealing with, even if that person wasn't a Christian, because it's true. The Law of Servanthood is a mentality; God can ask me for anything at any time and it's out of my account within the hour because it's not mine. It's been entrusted to me for His Kingdom.

> "Seek the Kingdom of God above all else, and live righteously, and he will give you everything you need."
>
> — MATTHEW 6:33

> "I will answer them before they even call to me. While they are still talking about their needs, I will go ahead and answer their prayers!"
>
> — ISAIAH 65:24

When you're a good servant, if you put God's kingdom first and all the things that pertain to you; God will hook you up. You'll never have to pray about needs. Before you imagine it, God will answer before you get the chance to pray it. Isaiah said that there's a class of people God answers before they even call. And while they're still speaking, God will hear.

For example, this is a small thing, but to me, it's big. There's a hat from Maui that I bought in January of 2021. I bought it, I liked it, and I still like it. But I thought, "Eventually, this hat will wear out, and it's only sold at that restaurant I like. I wish I'd bought a second one. Now I need to fly there and get a second one because they don't ship anything." I had that thought, and literally the next day, someone bought one in Maui and shipped it to me. It had to be supernatural!

My father is another example. He has been preaching for 45 years, and he certainly follows the law of servanthood. My dad is an old-school preacher, and to old-school preachers, everything is about the kingdom. They didn't have side interests; they just did ministry and church. Everything revolved around missions, gospel preaching, and soul winning.

My father was on a streak for many years; people would bring him something on his birthday, no matter where he was preaching. It was always something he wanted, like a brand new custom electric guitar or a $5,000 suit.

If you never tire of advancing God's kingdom, God will never tire of blessing you. As soon as you tire of advancing God's kingdom, God will tire of blessing you.

When Adalis and I launched Revival Today in 2007, it took all my faith and all my believing. My budget was $3,000 a month; it took a miracle for that to come in. Some months it didn't happen. It used to take all my faith for a month's worth of money, and now the same amount comes in every five hours. That's called increase.

It's funny how people say you shouldn't focus on money; you should focus on the Lord. When do you think I was more focused on money? When I needed $3000 a month, or now with $100,000 a week? The answer is when I needed $3000/month. It's not even a question. Back then, I prayed about money and believed for money. Now, I don't even think about it; I find out what the offerings are in the monthly report. It flows because it's an anointing, just like Elijah didn't have to worry about food.

It's actually the reverse of how people teach you. When you receive the financial anointing, money becomes something that doesn't concern you. Money is continually a concern when you don't have the financial anointing.

Back when I needed $3000 a month, if you had told me the day would come when I would need $100,000 a week, I would've immediately grabbed my chest and died of a heart attack.

God is a good God; He starts you off where you're at and then increases you as you build your faith. Reading the Word and attending meetings where you hear experts teach in your field increases your capacity to handle more talents for God's Kingdom. The Lord wouldn't have loaded me down with today's budget when I had less capacity. It's not because I was young; I hadn't developed my capacity enough yet. God brings you along, challenges your faith, and introduces new teachers who have revelation on His Word that you never saw before. Then, once you apply that revelation, it increases your capacity. The master can now entrust you, not just with one or two bags, but with five or ten bags based on your increased capacity. That's why preparation time is never wasted time. Study time's never wasted time because you're increasing your capacity to handle more. Where you are now is not where you'll finish.

There's always another level in God. Even if you've done very well in life, there will always be another level. Think of this, when God told Solomon in 1 Kings 3, "Solomon, I'm going to make you rich," Solomon was already rich. There's always another level in God. The more laser-focused you are on advancing God's Kingdom, the more the blessing of God follows without effort.

The largest church in the United States of America is Lakewood Church founded by John Osteen. He used to take one day a week in his office just to sign checks for missionaries; he gave tons of money. One church, one location, giving more money to missions than some entire denominations in the country. If you see the church now, they bought the building meant for the basketball team of that city.

What do you do personally to advance God's kingdom, financially? The average Christian can't point to one Kingdom endeavor in their lifetime where they've invested seriously.

You start where you're at. There are churches in Africa to which our ministry made significant contributions. I'm talking about giving

$20,000 when we had $30,000; it's significant to part with two-thirds of your net worth to help somebody else build their church.

It's significant because I'm not just helping somebody else build their church; I'm joining hands with Jesus to advance His kingdom. If you can see it like that; "I'm not helping my pastor build his church, I'm joining hands with Jesus to advance his Kingdom," you will be blessed. Have any of those churches paid me back? Have any of those churches sent me money when it was my turn to build a church? I don't know. I don't think so; I hope they didn't. Because Jesus said that if you help those who cannot help you, then your Heavenly Father will reward you.

If you only help those you know can help you, you're no different from the heathen. What you make happen for others, God makes happen for you. We've financially helped many, many churches with their building programs. Interestingly, now that it's come time for us to build our building, it's been the most pressure-free thing I've ever done. The law of servanthood; if I never tire of advancing God's kingdom, God will never tire of blessing me.

During the COVID outbreak, you heard people say the dumbest stuff about churches and buildings; "Maybe God's moving churches back into the family." I heard one minister—I use the word "minister" loosely—say, "I believe this is of God. God's moving the high priesthood away from the pastor and back to the father of the home."

They're stupid. A pastor is one of the five resurrection gifts Christ purchased for the earth through his death, burial, and resurrection. God likes church buildings, God likes them being built, and God likes big buildings full of people singing praise in unison to their Redeemer. When you get behind that, God gets behind you.

It's impossible not to take steps toward giving and not see visible proof that God is saying, "Good job, servant. You've been faithful in small things, and now I will show you another level." There's always another level in God.

I want you to ask yourself this; what notable contributions have you made to advancing God's kingdom, and when? Some people can't think of any, but you can always change that. Some people can think of a notable contribution, but they have to go back to 1993. It's a problem if you have to dig back 20-plus years for the last time something about God's Kingdom moved you. It's a problem, and that explains a pause in the blessing.

Too frequently, among people who have made a significant contribution in their life to the advancement of God's Kingdom, it's been off and on and not a continual thing. That's probably where people get the idea of "mountains and valleys," because they're inconsistent. When there is no seed, there is no harvest.

If there is sporadic seed, there is sporadic harvest. If there is little seed, there is little harvest. If there is abundant seed, there is abundant harvest. Continual seed brings continual harvest.

What notable contributions have you made to the advancement of God's kingdom? If you let that get in your heart, the money will never stop coming your way.

Of all the teachings you hear about God helping your dream come to pass, what would happen if you flipped it and realized that God has a dream He wants to see come to pass? *That all men be saved and come to a knowledge of the truth.*

Instead of asking God to help you fulfill your dream, ask God to empower you to fulfill His dream on the earth. Imagine making that flip. When you make that flip, the whole world will know it.

No one considers Billy Graham a prosperity preacher, but no ministry in America approaches his level of wealth. In making God's dream come to pass, their ministry had just under $700 million in reserve. You find very few corporations sitting on $700 million with no debt.

Seek ye first the advancement of the kingdom of God and His righteousness. When you do, all the things other men are working themselves to the bone to get will be added to you. This is the law of servanthood.

LAW SIX

THE LAW OF SOLUTION

If I create problems, I attract poverty. If I create solutions, I attract wealth. This is The Law of Solution. Everyone reading this knows at least one person considered a "problem" by this definition. People who create problems attract poverty because money is a reward for creating solutions. Money is not a mystery. Money is a reward for solving problems, and poverty is a reward for creating problems.

> Acquaint now thyself with him, and be at peace:
>   thereby good shall come unto thee.
> Receive, I pray thee, the law from his mouth, and lay
>   up his words in thine heart.
> If thou return to the Almighty, thou shalt be built up,
>   thou shalt put away iniquity far from thy
>   tabernacles.
> Then shalt thou lay up gold as dust, and the gold of
>   Ophir as the stones of the brooks.

> Yea, the Almighty shall be thy defence, and thou shalt have plenty of silver.
> For then shalt thou have thy delight in the Almighty, and shalt lift up thy face unto God.
> Thou shalt make thy prayer unto him, and he shall hear thee, and thou shalt pay thy vows.
> Thou shalt also decree a thing, and it shall be established unto thee: and the light shall shine upon thy ways.
> When men are cast down, then thou shalt say, There is lifting up; and he shall save the humble person.
> He shall deliver the island of the innocent: and it is delivered by the pureness of thine hands.
>
> — JOB 22:21-30 (KJV)

Is God saying that if you throw away your gold, He'll give you plenty of silver? No, God is saying if you put iniquity far from you, if you put sin far from you, if you return to the Lord, if you acquaint yourself with God, you will lay up gold. Your gold will start to multiply like it was dust, and the gold of Ophir as if it was worthless as stones in a brook.

As a Christian, you run on a different track than the rest of the world. When men are cast down, you can say, "There's a lifting up." Because you are a child of God, things are getting brighter for you!

If you are a child of God, you have this promise according to God's Word: you don't have to finish where you start. The Devil's not going to write the last chapter of your life, and He who began a good work in me will bring it to completion.

Now, if you're going to lay up gold like dust, you're not going to do that in your own strength. That's grace. That requires an imbuement of power called the anointing that operates in every area of life, including money. The anointing follows knowledge and understanding of the Word of God. Therefore, if the subject of Bible finance is unknown to you, or you don't understand it, or nobody's ever taught you, you'll never receive the anointing in that area. You'll never receive any anointing or anything from God that's not preached and taught to you.

> "Did you receive the Holy Spirit when you believed?"
> he [Paul] asked them.
> "No," they replied, "we haven't even heard that there
> is a Holy Spirit."
>
> — ACTS 19:2

The Devil can't stop the anointing, but he can get ministers to be ashamed of preaching and teaching what the Bible says. "Well, I believe in prosperity, but I don't preach it, or I don't talk about it from the pulpit because I don't want to be labeled a 'prosperity preacher.'"

Well, that's great. Now all your flock can struggle and become part of the debt system. Your flock can get vaccinated when they're told so they don't lose their jobs, because they don't know anything about divine provision. This is all because you won't teach them because you're ashamed of the Bible.

There's nothing the Bible says that I'm ashamed of. For example, I'm not ashamed of the Bible's stance on homosexuality, wealth, or healing.

I'd be ashamed to do the opposite and emphasize this too lightly. I would be ashamed to go through my whole ministry and never say anything bothersome to the spirit of the world.

If I create problems, I'll attract poverty. If I create solutions, I'll attract wealth. That is a lesson from the life of Joseph. Anywhere you put Joseph, he created solutions. If you made Joseph a slave, he was a slave who created so many solutions for his master that they had him stay in their home instead of making him stay with the other slaves. He was a solution-maker. They threw him in prison, and the Bible says Joseph created so many solutions that the warden didn't have anything to worry about except what he wanted to eat. Joseph even became assistant warden in the prison, which led to him becoming prime minister, second in command of the largest, most powerful nation of that time. He kept creating solutions until he rose to the second in command of his country.

I was on a trip with another pastor, and he got a phone call from somebody on staff at his church. He was far away from his church on a trip with me. The staff member said, "We can't find the key to open up part of the church we need to get into." While he was talking, I thought, if I was on vacation and I had a staff member do the same, that would be the end. You pay people to create solutions, not to create problems. Some people have individuals on their staff who do nothing but create problems. Of all the people who work at my ministry, there's not one person creating headaches; people just think about what they could do to create a solution, and they receive a reward—because that's scriptural.

Problem people are poor. And if they're not now, they soon will be because problem creators attract poverty. A solution creator attracts wealth.

Some people make a lot of money in a field of work called consulting. They don't really do anything; you tell them what you want to be done, and the problems you encounter, and they create a path to the solution. It's possible to train your mind to think toward solutions; there's always a way to do something. There's always a way to accomplish what you want to do.

There's a solution for every problem. For example, we started holding banquets in various cities to meet our followers who watch our content and read our books. During COVID, in one of the places where I was preaching, the state didn't allow indoor gatherings. No restaurants were willing to accommodate a group of people; you weren't allowed to have a table of more than six people.

I told the Revival Today staff, "Don't ever say that something can't be done." When people talk like that, I wonder if they've ever listened to anything I preach, because all things are possible to the one who believes. I mean, it's the central message of the Bible. That's not written for encouragement; that's an actual fact. All things are possible to him who believes; that means practical things too.

I needed a restaurant to host a large gathering of people in a state that was in lockdown. I could buy a restaurant, allow an exception for me and my group, then sell the restaurant when I'm finished. That's one way I could have done it.

But the easiest way to find a quick solution to any problem is to know an Italian person. Italian people always have cousins willing to bend a few rules to help somebody out. So, I knew an Italian person in New Jersey who is a friend of mine. I texted him and told him the problem. And I said, "Do you know anybody in New Jersey who owns a restaurant that will hook us up?" He said, "Oh, I have a cousin." His cousin opened his restaurant and told us to use the back entrance.

That problem, which originally had no solution, was solved in under five minutes by talking to a solution-minded person.

If I create solutions, I'll attract wealth. That man who created the solution for me is not in the restaurant business; he just has a mind that creates solutions. He's a multi, multi, multi-millionaire. You'll never meet a person who's earned wealth who thinks of limitations. They think of solutions.

I never heard one minister with a wealthy ministry say the government's not letting us meet. I heard wealthy ministers challenge the government or find a way to have their church meet. Wealthy people are solution minded. There's always a way out.

"We don't have any way to hire people right now." No, you do; just fix your brain. Quit blaming circumstances. If you use your brain to come up with solutions, you'll never lack wealth.

How you think and how you speak determines your limitation. This teaching is from the secular business world, and they don't even have God on their side. Why would you talk at a lower level and believe at a lower level than a secular businessperson when you're a person who's in covenant with God and carries the blessing of Abraham?

If you create problems, you'll attract poverty. If you accept problems, you'll stay in the middle. If you create solutions, you'll attract wealth.

LAW SEVEN

THE LAW OF ASSOCIATION

The company I keep determines what accompanies me; this is The Law of Association. You can't move forward tied to people committed to going backward. You can't move forward tied to people committed to remaining where they're at.

> Walk with the wise and become wise; associate with fools and get in trouble.
>
> — PROVERBS 13:20

Some people celebrate the fact that they've never grown. They say things like, "You know what I like about you? You're the same as when I knew you when you were 20." While they mean it as a compliment, it's a huge insult. You're supposed to grow. You're supposed to multiply. You're supposed to increase your capacity.

The average person's income is within a few percentage points of their three closest friends. You adopt the mentality, words, and thinking of the people you associate with. If you hang out with losers, you become a loser. If you hang out with people content with a job, a mortgage, and paying bills just to exist, you'll also operate like that. If you associate with great people who are builders, who take the land, you will acquire the same things they do. Their words have an effect on you. Their ideas change your mindset.

It's always funny to hear people say that they go to a dead church. They don't realize that in saying so, they're dead themselves. If you really were a person of faith, you wouldn't sit through even one Sunday service at a dead church. Who you associate with reveals who you are. Like-company attracts like-spirits.

There's a man on a worship team at a particular church. In my spirit, I have questions about him morally. There's another guy on a worship team at another church who I have those same questions about. I just looked on Instagram and saw they took a vacation together, just the two of them. Now all my suspicions are confirmed. Like spirits attract.

If you pass an accident on the street where somebody who owned a Rolls Royce got hit by an old car, would you laugh at the man with the Rolls Royce? "That's what you get. Serves you right." Do you have a harsh attitude toward wealthy people who have nice things? Or do you see somebody who's lived an uncommon life and wonder, what does he know that I don't know, that produced that life? "Why would anybody spend that much money on a car? Why would anybody spend that much money on a house?" You can never attain a place in life if you hate the people in that place.

Could I have accomplished what I did during the COVID lockdown, defying government restrictions, if I was tied to a denomination that disagreed with my choices? Even if I had kept taking the course of action I did, it would have discouraged me. I probably would have backed off some. You can't be a warrior tied to people who don't want to fight. But who am I tied to instead? I'm tied in the ministry to an overseer fighting harder than me, who got arrested. I didn't get arrested. He kept his church open and took a stand for the country. So, I wasn't getting phone calls telling me to back down. I was getting phone calls telling me, "Good job; keep doing what you're doing."

Obviously, you have to interact with people you disagree with every day. That's life. But I'm talking about close associations. How do you associate with champions?

So, what do you do? Just quit hanging out with your old friends and drop by Warren Buffett's house? Go meet Franklin Graham? Ask if he wants to play miniature golf with you? No, those may not be options. But today, everything is easily accessible through YouTube, Instagram, podcasts, etc. Great people have put their wisdom out for you to receive it.

Right now, you're reading from someone you respect and want to know what they have to say. If you make that behavior a lifestyle, it'll change your life. Go to events where great people are speaking. Listen to new things and go to new places where champions gather to learn how to become a conqueror. Don't sit back with the ten spies discussing how you cannot take the land. Get with the Joshua and Caleb's of your generation. Who are they? Find out who they are.

I make it my business to find out who the top ministers in the world are, go to where they are, and obtain their books and receive from them. I've had them all lay hands on me. I flew to Nigeria to meet Bishop Oyedepo and be in his building. I wanted to see and be in a church sanctuary that seated 50,000 people. I knew it would do something for me. It's one thing to hear about it or watch it on video, it's another thing to see it in person.

This opens your spirit up to what's possible. You don't hear people say, well, it's tough to have a church of over 500 people. No, it's not. I've seen a choir loft that seats 5,000. It changes you. Look at all the great men of God who built great churches; they all went to see David Yonggi Cho in South Korea and see the world's largest church. It changed their ministry because you can never arrive at a future you've not seen. God had to take Abraham out and say: *Look at the stars; that's how your descendants will be.*

Before I ever flew on my own jet, Rodney Howard-Browne took me on his jet. I saw it's possible. I quit hanging around with people who talked about expensive gas and started being around people who have personal aircraft. It changes your mind.

You will never hear somebody with a private aircraft say, "I can't believe gas is $4 a gallon." They're way past that. You can't attain Abrahamic-level wealth, Job-level wealth, or Solomon-level wealth while hanging around people who spend two hours on Saturday clipping coupons to save twenty dollars. What are you going to do with $20? In the two hours you spent saving $20, do you know what else you could have been doing that would have generated far more money?

Many of us were raised in homes where producing money was never thought about or talked about. Everything was about saving money. But God didn't say I'll bless you, and you'll learn how to get good deals and save money. God said, "I'll give you the power to create wealth."

One way to associate with champions is to ask the Lord to bring great people into your path. In my twenties, I went on a 21-day fast because I had read the story of how God knit Lester Sumrall to Howard Carter. This relationship transformed Lester Sumrall's life from a young guy holding revivals without connection, to traveling the world. Howard

Carter was the head of the Assemblies of God in England, which was how Lester Sumrall met Smith Wigglesworth.

I said, "Lord, I don't have anybody like that in my life. Can you give me a Howard Carter, like you gave Lester Sumrall?" On day 17 of the fast, Rodney Howard-Browne called me. If he didn't have such a distinct voice, I would've thought it was somebody playing a prank on me. My dad and his three brothers are all in the ministry, and they're all good ministers. So, I said, "This is Jonathan. Did you mean to call one of my uncles or my dad?" He said, "No, actually, I got your number from your uncle to call you." I said, "Why?" I was living in an 800-square-foot apartment. I had no money. "What do you need to talk to me for?" He said, "I felt quickened in my spirit by the Lord to call you and invite you to come down to Florida to spend a few days with me." I said, "I'll be there tomorrow."

Adalis was at the grocery store. I called her and said, "Put the groceries back. We're going to Florida right now." She said, "Oh, okay. I'll be right home." That's my wife. No explanation was required. We had about $900 in the bank. I bought two coach tickets for her and I. God opened the door. Many people still miss it because they delay, even when God opens a door.

The opportunity of a lifetime has to be seized in the lifetime of the opportunity. "Okay, Dr. Rodney. Well, maybe I'll come down and see you the next time I'm in Florida." No. If he was quickened in his spirit at that moment, the time to move was immediate.

If you ask God to do something and He does it, God's not going to say, "Oh yeah, but you know, that's going to be $600 to fly down there. So, you know. You need to use wisdom."

Get moving. Stop saying what you don't have and ask God for what you need. Relationships open doors. You can pray for those things. If you don't have them, you're not praying for them. God answered that prayer quickly, just over two weeks.

That began in 2011, a turning point in my life and ministry where Adalis and I were tied in with Dr. Rodney. The exact thing that happened with Lester Sumrall and Howard Carter happened with me. Being around Dr. Rodney, I began to meet great men and women in the body of Christ from all over the world. I had never preached in South Africa before meeting Dr. Rodney Howard-Browne. Through that divine connection, television opened up to me in South Africa, and then in America. That divine connection was produced by my desire to move forward and not stay where I was. The law of association.

Who are your three closest relationships outside of your spouse, your children, and your parents? Are they people who are below you, and pulling you down? Are they the same as you, so you can justify why none of you grow? Or do you have close relationships with people far ahead of you, who challenge you to be greater? Have you purposefully chosen relationships with people less than you just to feel good about yourself? "You know, I'm the only one of my friends still in full-time ministry." Then you need to pick new friends. Pursue relationships with people ahead of you who have done more than you, who know more than you. That requires security. Insecure people can't do that.

I met Bishop Oyedepo through Dr. Rodney Howard-Browne. I did not say one word for 40 minutes. I wouldn't have said one word the entire time if Bishop Oyedepo didn't look me over and say, "What's your name?" I answered him. "You're a minister as well?" I acknowledged him. "Nice to meet you." You should be quiet and listen when great men talk. When God gives you access to someone you deem great, honor the relationship.

Some people have great men of God in their lives who are in the ministry and expect that man to give them money. They don't care about his wisdom. They don't care about what he knows that produces money. They're just hoping he blesses them with a watch. If Elisha was an American minister and Elijah said, "Ask me for anything, what would you like me to give you?" He would have said, "I'd like your watch. I'd like your robe. I want that cool chariot that you have." Some people don't understand that the true treasure is what's in that man's spirit, that is what produces all those material things. They miss it. They miss out.

Everything I give to the ministers that the Lord has placed in my life is because I respect them, and because they challenge me. It's not for them to hopefully pay me back one day. Some of the ministers I've sown to can't pay me back. I'm doing it to honor them. I'm doing it to keep a spiritual connection.

Honor them, honor them financially, bless them. Follow their ministry. What are they doing right now? What are they believing God for? Ask God how you can help them accomplish their dream in their ministry like Elisha did for Elijah. Then what you make happen for others, God makes happen for you.

I don't hang out with ministers who discuss other ministries; I hang out with ministers who are being discussed by other ministries. "What do you think about Benny Hinn?" I think I'd rather hang out with him than hang out with people that talk about him. I'd rather be a person that's discussed than a person who discusses other people.

You can't take the promised land while hanging out with the 10 spies. You can only take the promised land by hanging out with Joshua and Caleb. And your friends are either 10 spy friends, or they're Joshua and Caleb friends. That's the law of association.

LAW EIGHT

THE LAW OF COVENANT LAND OWNERSHIP

You have the same blessing as Abraham; everything God promised to Abraham now belongs to you; this is The Law of Covenant Land Ownership.

> After Lot had gone, the Lord said to Abram, "Look as far as you can see in every direction—north and south, east and west. I am giving all this land, as far as you can see, to you and your descendants as a permanent possession. And I will give you so many descendants that, like the dust of the earth, they cannot be counted! Go and walk through the land in every direction, for I am giving it to you."
> So Abram moved his camp to Hebron and settled near the oak grove belonging to Mamre. There he built another altar to the Lord.
>
> — GENESIS 13:14-18

> In the same way, "Abraham believed God, and God counted him as righteous because of his faith." The real children of Abraham, then, are those who put their faith in God.
>
> What's more, the Scriptures looked forward to this time when God would make the Gentiles right in his sight because of their faith. God proclaimed this good news to Abraham long ago when he said, "All nations will be blessed through you." So all who put their faith in Christ share the same blessing Abraham received because of his faith.
>
> But those who depend on the law to make them right with God are under his curse, for the Scriptures say, "Cursed is everyone who does not observe and obey all the commands that are written in God's Book of the Law." So it is clear that no one can be made right with God by trying to keep the law. For the Scriptures say, "It is through faith that a righteous person has life." This way of faith is very different from the way of law, which says, "It is through obeying the law that a person has life."
>
> But Christ has rescued us from the curse pronounced by the law. When he was hung on the cross, he took upon himself the curse for our wrongdoing. For it is written in the Scriptures, "Cursed is everyone who is hung on a tree." Through Christ Jesus, God has blessed the Gentiles with the same blessing he promised to Abraham, so that we who are believers might receive the promised Holy Spirit through faith.
>
> — GALATIANS 3:6-14

> And now that you belong to Christ, you are the true children of Abraham. You are his heirs, and God's promise to Abraham belongs to you.
>
> — GALATIANS 3:29

What did God promise Abraham? In Genesis 13:14, God gave land to Abraham. God gave land to everyone He ever made a covenant with in the Bible.

There are two comedians I like: Jerry Seinfeld and Colin Quinn. Jerry is Jewish. Colin Quinn is Irish, or as the Bible calls it, Gentile. They both started out in New York, and they both moved to Los Angeles at the same point in their careers. Colin Quinn said he met up with Jerry Seinfeld a few months later and said, "Man, it was hard finding a place in Los Angeles. I ended up renting," and he told him what apartment he rented. He asked, "Were you able to get an apartment?" Jerry Seinfeld said, "I bought that apartment." Colin Quinn said, "What do you mean you bought that apartment? I've never heard of that before." Jerry Seinfeld replied, "Jews don't rent." That's a direct quote. His words, not mine.

If you're a Gentile, which I am, you are raised to believe in credit, debt, and renting—the opposite of the Bible. The Bible says *I'll make you the head and not the tail*. You can do better in life by fully believing the first five books of the Bible than by sort of believing all 66 books. Jews don't rent. Jerry Seinfeld was obviously raised with a mentality that we don't rent; we buy. The Bible gives you the exact same mentality if you read it correctly. But because most Christians are more American than they are Christian, more English than they are Christian, and more South African than Christian, they actually adopt their culture's view on money and land ownership instead of the Bible's.

While growing up, I received advice from preachers like, "You need to have a good credit score to borrow money." Until I was about 26, I was never around preachers who conveyed this part of the Bible; you'll be the financial head and not the financial tail. Are you taking the Bible out of context when you apply the verse that says you'll be the head and not the tail to finances? No, because, in the same passage, it says you will lend to many, but thou shall not borrow. Financial headship is part of your covenant right. Part of your finance headship is the law of covenant land ownership. You will rent land to others; you will not pay rent for land. You will build fine homes to live in. You won't pay rent to use other people's fine homes.

You say, "Man, but that seems impossible from where I'm at." When I first heard this, it felt impossible to me too. And within 18 months, I owned a dentist's office, two apartments, and an office building for our ministry. I had never owned any land in 37 years, commercial or private. I never owned a home. We leased our business property. As soon as I saw there was never anybody in the Bible that God made a covenant with who He didn't turn land over to, it clicked in my mind. Now the land keeps coming into my possession. Because the Christian prevails by revelation. Not by striving, not by trying, not by saving. The Christian conquers through revelation.

When you see in the Bible that something belongs to you, when you understand the way you're living is anti-covenant or unscriptural, it flips. Me paying rent to people is not part of my covenant. People paying rent to me is part of my covenant. As soon as I saw that it was unscriptural and needed to flip, it flipped.

> My people are destroyed for lack of knowledge:
> because thou hast rejected knowledge, I will also
> reject thee, that thou shalt be no priest to me:

seeing thou hast forgotten the law of thy God, I
will also forget thy children.

— HOSEA 4:6 (KJV)

The first gift God ever gave to man was land. The word "land" is used in the Bible 1,641 times. It's reasonably important to God. Every battle and war being fought on planet earth is over land and border disputes. It's a serious thing to own land. It's part of your covenant relationship with God to own land. I don't care if you're 23 or 63; age does not matter when it comes to this. It's when you make the discovery. I would still be paying rent and leasing if I never made this discovery in the Bible. The righteous shall possess the land. God talked about land all the time in the Bible. God gave instructions in the Bible for people to go and take land.

> Moses continued, "Then the LORD said, 'Now get moving! Cross the Arnon Gorge. Look, I will hand over to you Sihon the Amorite, king of Heshbon, and I will give you his land. Attack him and begin to occupy the land.'"
>
> — DEUTERONOMY 2:24

That's land transfer. God is somewhat land-obsessed. God can decide in heaven about the land that somebody owns and give it to you. He did it all throughout the Bible.

It's a spiritual battle. Satan desires to keep you a borrower and a tenant. Satan's objectives for your life are the opposite of God's desires. Christ came that you might have life and have it more abundantly. Satan came to steal, kill, and destroy. God said: *I'll give you land, and I'll make you lend only and never borrow.* If Satan has his way, you'll borrow only and never have any leftover to lend. So there is a satanic buffering to keep you in the position of renter, tenant, and borrower.

God wants to make you the lender and never the borrower, including in the area of land. My friend Ms. Murdoch said, "God gave my grandpa lots of land. He planted churches and had rental property. My grandfather was blessed." God is no respecter of persons. What God does for one, He'll do for anybody that does what that person did.

Adalis and I like to take our vacations in Scottsdale, Arizona, because it feels very peaceful. There are some places that trouble my spirit. I don't mind going there to preach, but I could never go there to relax. Scottsdale, Arizona, feels extremely peaceful to me.

After going there for several years, I wondered why this place felt so peaceful. I told Adalis, "I bet the town has a good history, how it was founded, and why."

Dale is an old word for farm, so Scottsdale is Scott's farm. Winfield Scott secured that land back when it was worthless desert land in the 1800s. He was a pastor during his time serving in the military. He had a church in Kansas with only 12 members and built it into a church of 250 people. He then built two offsite campuses for those who couldn't travel that far. He was a good man of God.

I found in his book that Winfield Scott's grandmother had a farm, and her church needed more land, so she gave them a large portion of her acreage to use for the church. Two generations later, the government gifted a massive amount of acreage to Winfield Scott. He received intelligence from being in the military that a reservoir of water was coming from California into what's now Scottsdale. The purpose of the water was to transform worthless desert land into lush farmland. His grandmother sowed acres, and her grandson was given a town.

If that doesn't cement the law of sowing and reaping into your mind, I don't know what will. Not only does it work in the area of land, but it's actually transgenerational, as with this story. What you're doing now will affect future generations.

I don't know of anything more impactful to future generations than land ownership. Imagine the difference in my daughter's life if she has to get an apartment after graduating, or if her father can gift her a few acres and a home. We're talking about giving somebody a 25 to 30-year head start in life by deciding to break out of being the borrower, not the lender. To break out of being below to being above instead. To break out from being beneath to being the head.

People are reading this who nobody in their family has ever owned land or a home. Everybody rents, and everybody borrows. But it only takes one person to be the first in their family to break out, and then it affects future generations. It is improbable to own land and a home and then go back to renting; you'd have to make some serious mistakes.

You can miss everything before and after this, but don't miss this—Everyone God made a covenant with, He turned land over to them. Adam, the Adamic Covenant, He gave him the Garden of Eden. Then, in Genesis 8 and 9, you can see what God said to Noah when the ark settled.

> Then God said to Noah, "Leave the boat, all of you—
> you and your wife, and your sons and their
> wives. Release all the animals—the birds, the
> livestock, and the small animals that scurry along

the ground—so they can be fruitful and multiply
throughout the earth."

So Noah, his wife, and his sons and their wives left the
boat. And all of the large and small animals and
birds came out of the boat, pair by pair.

Then Noah built an altar to the Lord, and there he
sacrificed as burnt offerings the animals and birds
that had been approved for that purpose. And
the Lord was pleased with the aroma of the
sacrifice and said to himself, "I will never again
curse the ground because of the human race, even
though everything they think or imagine is bent
toward evil from childhood. I will never again
destroy all living things. As long as the earth
remains, there will be planting and harvest, cold
and heat, summer and winter, day and night."

— GENESIS 8:15-22

Then God blessed Noah and his sons and told them,
"Be fruitful and multiply. Fill the earth. All the
animals of the earth, all the birds of the sky, all the
small animals that scurry along the ground, and all
the fish in the sea will look on you with fear and
terror. I have placed them in your power. I have
given them to you for food, just as I have given
you grain and vegetables. But you must never eat
any meat that still has the lifeblood in it.

"And I will require the blood of anyone who takes
another person's life. If a wild animal kills a

person, it must die. And anyone who murders a fellow human must die. If anyone takes a human life, that person's life will also be taken by human hands. For God made human beings in his own image. Now be fruitful and multiply, and repopulate the earth."

Then God told Noah and his sons, "I hereby confirm my covenant with you and your descendants, and with all the animals that were on the boat with you—the birds, the livestock, and all the wild animals—every living creature on earth. Yes, I am confirming my covenant with you. Never again will floodwaters kill all living creatures; never again will a flood destroy the earth."

Then God said, "I am giving you a sign of my covenant with you and with all living creatures, for all generations to come. I have placed my rainbow in the clouds. It is the sign of my covenant with you and with all the earth. When I send clouds over the earth, the rainbow will appear in the clouds, and I will remember my covenant with you and with all living creatures. Never again will the floodwaters destroy all life. When I see the rainbow in the clouds, I will remember the eternal covenant between God and every living creature on earth." Then God said to Noah, "Yes, this rainbow is the sign of the covenant I am confirming with all the creatures on earth."

The sons of Noah who came out of the boat with their father were Shem, Ham, and Japheth. (Ham is the father of Canaan.) From these three sons of Noah came all the people who now populate the earth.

> After the flood, Noah began to cultivate the ground, and he planted a vineyard.
>
> — GENESIS 9:1-20

The covenants tied to Noah, Abraham, Adam, and Moses all intertwined with the concept of land in significant ways.

We already read in Genesis 13, *Look as far as you can see in the north, south, east, and west. For I am giving all of this land to you and your descendants forever.* That's covenant land. That's why you should be careful if you're a world leader making plans against the nation of Israel. The bottom line is that they are the descendants of Abraham. And God said: *I'm giving that land to you and your descendants forever.* God loves that nation, and God loves those people, and that land is a gift from him to them. You should never forget that.

The New Covenant that Christ opened up for believers involves land. What land is God going to give to the believers? In the 1,000-year millennial reign of Christ, all of it. Believers will own the earth, and then a new Jerusalem and a new earth. The New Covenant involves land.

> All the believers were united in heart and mind. And they felt that what they owned was not their own, so they shared everything they had. The apostles testified powerfully to the resurrection of the Lord Jesus, and God's great blessing was upon them all. There were no needy people among them, because those who owned land or houses would sell them and bring the money to the apostles to give to those in need.

For instance, there was Joseph, the one the apostles nicknamed Barnabas (which means "Son of Encouragement"). He was from the tribe of Levi and came from the island of Cyprus. He sold a field he owned and brought the money to the apostles.

But there was a certain man named Ananias who, with his wife, Sapphira, sold some property. He brought part of the money to the apostles, claiming it was the full amount. With his wife's consent, he kept the rest.

Then Peter said, "Ananias, why have you let Satan fill your heart? You lied to the Holy Spirit, and you kept some of the money for yourself. The property was yours to sell or not sell, as you wished. And after selling it, the money was also yours to give away. How could you do a thing like this? You weren't lying to us but to God!"

As soon as Ananias heard these words, he fell to the floor and died. Everyone who heard about it was terrified. Then some young men got up, wrapped him in a sheet, and took him out and buried him.

About three hours later his wife came in, not knowing what had happened. Peter asked her, "Was this the price you and your husband received for your land?"

"Yes," she replied, "that was the price."

And Peter said, "How could the two of you even think of conspiring to test the Spirit of the Lord like this? The young men who buried your husband are just outside the door, and they will carry you out, too."

Instantly, she fell to the floor and died. When the young men came in and saw that she was dead,

> they carried her out and buried her beside her husband. Great fear gripped the entire church and everyone else who heard what had happened.
>
> — ACTS 4:32-5:11

This passage was all about land. That's the New Covenant.

Everyone God made a covenant with in the Bible, he turned physical land over to them. Abraham, Noah, Moses, and believers. I want you to confess this over yourself; 'I am in covenant with God. The New Covenant, signed by the blood of Jesus. That's the covenant I have with God. Abraham had a covenant with God. Adam had a covenant with God. Noah had a covenant with God. Moses had a covenant with God. I have a covenant with God. And everyone God was in covenant with, he turned land over to them.'

Get these things in your heart—Just as it's your right to be free from sin, it's your right to be baptized in the Holy Ghost, all because of your covenant with God. It's your right to be healed. It's your right to be prosperous. It is your covenant right to own land.

> The godly will possess the land and will live there forever.
>
> — PSALM 37:29

Land acquisition is spiritual. Land acquisition is spiritual because spirits are territorial, and territorial spirits can't operate on land you own. You can either bring your little charismatic women's group up on a mountain with flags and acoustic guitars and try to pray the spirits off the land, or you can just buy the land. When it's yours, they leave; they can't be where the believer is because light drives out darkness, darkness doesn't drive out light. I choose option B. I don't know what went on in my office building before I got here, but it doesn't go on now. I don't know what went on in the building I bought across the street before I bought it, but it doesn't go on now. There's prayer here, continual prayer. When you buy the land, no spirits have to be rebuked. It's yours. You go there, they clear out.

Some churches rent their building from nightclubs. They rent a nightclub to have their Sunday morning service. I don't know how anybody can't see how backward that is. You have places built on strippers, cocaine, and alcohol, allowing a church to use their building for pay. You have a wicked person that, under a curse, has risen up to a place to acquire property and land. Then they lend it to a church, while the church is living righteously and can't understand why they should acquire the land and building.

I'm sure some consider me controversial for teaching this. But it's controversial if you can't see that God doesn't want you to rent your church space from a nightclub, sweeping the cocaine off the floor to set up the communion trays.

My people are destroyed for lack of knowledge. If something's not taught to people, they'll never have it. People won't teach you about land ownership and property acquisition as part of your biblical covenant. They actually make it seem like it's part of your covenant to be poor, in need, and struggling. It's unscriptural. Abraham didn't rent, Abraham owned. Land acquisition is spiritual because spirits are territorial, and territorial spirits can't operate on land you own.

It takes an anointing to acquire land and property. You can acquire it without the anointing, but that's why many pastors have heart attacks or resign within 18 months of getting the land. After doing so much to acquire land and build a church, can you imagine quitting six months later because it was so taxing? After it's finally completed, you don't even feel like preaching in the church God gave you. That's demonic. But the anointing makes things flow smoothly. The anointing is likened in the Bible to oil. What does oil do in an engine? It makes the parts run smoothly; it reduces friction and absorbs the heat. That's what the anointing does. It attracts wealth, makes everything run smoothly, and absorbs the friction and heat that burn other people out.

Land acquisition needs to be done through anointing. Consider this—My uncle Ted Shuttlesworth visits my broadcast, and as we leave for lunch, he looks at the building across the street. I didn't own the building at that time, but he prophecies, "You've outgrown your current building. That building is your next move." We informed him that it had just been sold less than six months ago. He replies, "When you find out that the sale for the building falls through, that's your sign that it belongs to you."

Six days later, the owner of the building calls and says, "The people that bought the building next to you have not made one payment since they bought it. I'm going back to repossess it today, and for some reason, I was thinking of you guys. I know you just bought the other building, but I can make it happen if you'd like that one too." And we bought it. There were no offerings, no fundraising campaign, no coloring in a red thermometer, no mortgage, and no bank involvement because there's an anointing to acquire land.

In that building, a dentist leases some of the property. I could not afford to take my wife to the dentist to get her teeth fixed when she was 26 and in severe tooth pain, and now I own a dentist's building. God can turn your situation around from not being able to afford to go to the dentist to owning a dentist's office. That's what God does. Most testimonies are, "I couldn't afford to go to the dentist, then praise the Lord, someone paid for it for me." But you can go so much higher. You can go as high in life as you allow your faith to take you.

Our ministry's not just debt-free. Our ministry has never had any debt to be free from. We paid cash for every move we've made, including this church that we're building. We even bought the excavation equipment instead of renting it. I couldn't afford a car in the past, and now I have earth-moving equipment. That's by the anointing because it's the same me. Everything starts to line up when you understand who you are, what belongs to you, and your covenant with God.

Dr. John G. Lake was used mightily by God in healing under John Alexander Dowie's teachings, and I'll never forget what he said. "When I saw from the Bible that sickness was not a part of life, that sickness was from Satan, not God, every fiber of my being rose up to reject it." Before he read that, he felt, "Eh, wives get sick, children get sick and die. That's just how it goes." Back then, you'd lose half your kids before they turned 12 or 13. A husband and wife would have eight kids, and five would survive. But then, he said, "When I saw in the Bible that sickness is of the Devil, everything in my being rose up to throw it out." The same thing can happen in borrowing and renting. That's not where I belong. When that conviction rises up in your soul, everything starts turning around.

You tap into the anointing by revelation. When I read Psalm 37:29, that's when everything turned around. I was teaching from Psalm 37 on a different topic; what kept popping out at me was how many times it talked about land.

> Don't worry about the wicked or envy those who do wrong. For like grass, they soon fade away. Like spring flowers, they soon wither.
> Trust in the Lord and do good. Then you will live safely in the land and prosper. Take delight in the Lord, and he will give you your heart's desires.
> Commit everything you do to the Lord. Trust him, and

> he will help you. He will make your innocence radiate like the dawn, and the justice of your cause will shine like the noonday sun.
> Be still in the presence of the Lord, and wait patiently for him to act. Don't worry about evil people who prosper or fret about their wicked schemes.
> Stop being angry! Turn from your rage! Do not lose your temper— it only leads to harm. For the wicked will be destroyed, but those who trust in the Lord will possess the land.
>
> — PSALM 37:1-9

> Those the Lord blesses will possess the land, but those he curses will die.
>
> — PSALM 37:22

> Day by day the Lord takes care of the innocent, and they will receive an inheritance that lasts forever. They will not be disgraced in hard times; even in famine they will have more than enough.
>
> — PSALM 37:18-19

How many more do you want to read? Now, somebody make a case from the Bible about why I should have to pay rent. Someone might say, "Yeah, I know, but I don't know how that can happen while I rent." Yeah, so did I when I read it, and then it flipped.

Quit seeing things through the lens of where you are now and start seeing what the Bible says belongs to you. It's no different from when people first come to the altar and get saved. They have a hard time. They say things like, "All I do is drink and do drugs. I don't know how I can ever not live that way," and you're trying to explain to them, "Yeah, but you're born again now. You have a new covenant. That's not you anymore. You don't have to live like that. You have power over those things." But they insist by saying, "I know, but it's just that I smoke every day." They're going by who they were, not who they are. You're trying to get them to see who they are. It's the same revelation as this.

The Word carries the power to create the solution. God's Word doesn't just show you solutions, when you receive God's word, it carries power to create the solution. You tap into the anointing by revelation.

When you acquire land, you please God by doing what a righteous man is created to do. The righteous shall possess the land. God loves property acquisition. When you heard pastors talk about how church buildings aren't important during the pandemic, you were listening to a devil. They're stupid people. God loves churches being built. Part of the purpose of a righteous man is to possess the land; it's a function of your righteousness.

God set things up for us to play from ahead and not behind. Land ownership results in setting up your city council structures and school boards; the landowners have power.

There was a time when you didn't vote without owning land. No one even cared what your opinion was if you didn't own land.

The message of the Bible is that God has empowered you to overthrow the wicked out of the land, spiritually, by the authority that

God's given you. This is without ever firing a shot, without ever throwing a punch. You can pray them out. You can bind them. You can curse their plans, like we've done in America, and it blows it all out.

We are not on this earth to be dominated. We were put on this earth and have been given dominion in this life. There's no domination without land ownership. If I didn't own land, my ministry would have been shut down last year during COVID because they shut down the office park in which we had been leasing property. But God made a plan to give us our own buildings that can't be shut down, so the Gospel can go forth.

Land ownership is dominion. Land ownership is power. Land ownership has been given to you by God. It's not a light thing. It's part of your covenant, and it's time to make up your mind. "I'm done being the tail. I'm done being beneath. I'm done being below. I make up my mind today. I'm going to operate in the full covenant of God, and I don't give two poos what the government thinks about it or what the established government-bought religious order thinks about it. I am blessed by God, and those He blesses shall possess the land."

LAW NINE

THE LAW OF THE FAMILY

The Law of the Family is important in life and in the Bible, and it's extremely important to God.

> But those who won't care for their relatives, especially those in their own household, have denied the true faith. Such people are worse than unbelievers.
>
> — 1 TIMOTHY 5:8

God didn't create the family as a concession to sin. It's not like Adam was single in the garden, then he sinned, and God said, "Guys are going to have sex, so I better hurry up and create a framework that won't cause problems." No. The family existed before the fall. God is a "family" God; God instituted the family. The attacks of the Devil in our nation are against the family. A family can survive without a nation, but a nation can't survive without the family.

It's very important to deal with this law when it comes to wealth creation and the laws that govern the financial anointing. I've broken the law of the family into nine subpoints to help you better understand.

STABILITY, PRESERVATION, AND ENJOYMENT OF WEALTH

The family is a unit created by God. This isn't the only thing it provides, but among other things, it provides stability for your wealth, protection for your wealth, preservation for your wealth, and enjoyment of your wealth.

Solomon—the richest man who ever lived—said there's nothing more pleasing than sitting at the table and eating with your family or taking your family on trips. Your brain's been messed up by television shows if you think that when you get rich, the real fun is to meet up with a bunch of strangers at a nightclub, but it's not. You rarely get shot with a nine-millimeter while eating with your family at a table. There are seldom people in the next room being loud and obnoxious. The real pleasure of life is blessing your family and enjoying life with your family.

Let's break down this definition I gave under point number one; the family provides a unit for stability for your wealth. It's hard to accumulate wealth when you're swapping out your wife every seven years, paying divorce costs, and losing 50% of your wealth in the settlement. The family provides a platform where God will build your wealth. A foundation. If you have an unstable family, there won't be stability for your money. The family is a unit God created to provide stability and protection for your wealth.

Not too many years ago, a politician had to pay $130,000 to a prostitute so she wouldn't tell anybody that he slept with her. The politician's wife was pregnant, so he decided to meet with this prostitute. It cost him $130,000 for her to "stay quiet," and she ended up talking anyway.

For the most part, your family's not likely to turn on you. I have family that works for us in the ministry. Even if they get mad at me and don't like me anymore, they're probably not going to run to the newspaper and make up stuff about me. Strangers do that. Some people's family members do that too, but most families provide stability. They're not going to look to hurt you. They'll do it personally in a conversation with you if they do. They're not going to go and elicit help to take out a fellow family member.

The mafia understood this principle. That's what made them run strong for 110 years. They operated with the principles of family. Italians would only allow other Italians in; somebody had to vouch for you. They weren't just a loose group of criminals; they called themselves a family. Obviously, it's perverted, but the principle remains. They weren't bringing strangers in. You shouldn't have strangers live in your home. Your home is a place for family, immediate family.

Stability and protection. If you marry a godly wife, she'll protect you. You don't have to pay her to be quiet. The family is a unit created by God to provide stability, protection, and preservation of wealth. Remember Abraham? "I'm an old man and I don't have a son. I don't have anyone to be my heir." He was already thinking about preserving his wealth; he was thinking about transgenerational wealth. The family provides a structure for you to perpetuate your wealth. My ceiling will be my daughter's floor, she will start with things that took me 35 years to obtain. That's a Godly system. Isaac re-dug the wells his father had dug. Abraham left land to Isaac. Isaac left land to Jacob along with flocks, cattle, and other wealth.

The purpose of wealth is to create pleasurable experiences for yourself and others, and chiefly among the others, is family. The family is a unit created by God to provide stability, protection, preservation, and enjoyment of wealth. So, you perpetuate wealth through family, rather than turn it all over to the government when you die. What's the point of having money if it doesn't bring enjoyment? It's nice to bless your family; it's written all through Ecclesiastes.

You say, "What about the kingdom of God?" When you tell your pastor that the new roof he's putting on the church—that's going to cost $150,000—you're going to take care of it. Now you've created a pleasurable experience for that man. Wealth gives you opportunities to create pleasurable experiences in life for yourself and other people.

If I spot a minister in my service who's a good man of God, I'll call him up to the front and have him tell everybody about his ministry. I'll give him that night's offering. Why? I don't need it. I couldn't have done that when I needed this week's offering to pay next week's bills. When you go into overflow and an abundance of wealth, you have opportunities to create pleasurable experiences for yourself and others. Look for who you can bless, not for who can bless you.

A BREAKDOWN IN FAMILY WILL BREAKDOWN YOUR WEALTH

A family breakdown will destroy your wealth. So, if you care about wealth, you should care about your family. It's not one or the other;

wealth allows you to bless your family and create pleasurable experiences. Having a stable family prevents things from eating away at your wealth.

Divorce will cost you a lot of money. If you lost 50% of what you have in the stock market in a day, you would consider that a major crash. That's what divorce will do to your assets. Even if you signed a prenuptial agreement—which most people haven't—divorce lawyers are expensive. If you make the lady mad enough, she goes to the paper and defames you in the media, defames your business. It's a mistake.

It's the same with addicted children if you let your kids fall into drugs. I met a man when I was preaching. He said, "I'm a wealthy business owner, and my son is on heroin. Between lawyers for what he does while he's on drugs, rehab, and methadone, he's bleeding out my personal money and the money from my business." God delivered that man's son that same day, and he was very thankful. So that's why the Devil tries to attack the family, to stop the flow of your finances.

> Better a dry crust eaten in peace than a house filled with feasting—and conflict.
>
> — PROVERBS 17:1

> A bowl of vegetables with someone you love is better than steak with someone you hate.
>
> — PROVERBS 15:17

A BREAKDOWN IN FAMILY MAKES WEALTH POINTLESS

A breakdown in family makes your wealth pointless. Ever heard of an old rich miser? They're rich, but they don't have any outlet for enjoyment. The money actually becomes an end to itself, a perversion of how God created things to work. Then you start loving your money and caring about money more than you care about people.

I guarantee you, I had a better time coming back to Adalis in a 600-square-foot apartment than many people who live in mansions and hate being home. It's one reason for staying at work so long; some people hate being with their wives, and their children bring them no joy while they bring no joy to their children. Their home is a million-dollar place they avoid at all costs.

A breakdown in family makes your wealth pointless, but let's focus on the positive. If you build your family such that you enjoy their company and they enjoy your company, there's a purpose for your wealth. Like anything else you build, family requires investment. Spending quality time with your wife is extremely valuable. Reading stories to your children from the Bible before going to bed and praying with them is also extremely valuable.

Some years ago, I met a man whose wife—although he made a lot of money—was growing miserable. Still, he wouldn't spend any of it or let her spend anything. His reason for not spending it was not because he was cheap. It sounded noble when he said, "I'm saving up to buy a house."

One day I told him, "Take your wife on vacation."

He replied, "I will once we build that house."

I said, "Let me ask you a question. What good is it to have a nice, big, beautiful house and a wife that has checked out of your relationship, even if she doesn't divorce you?"

Some people live together, but they've checked out of the relationship. There's no love or attachment between the couple. This is where I differ from some people who teach stewardship. You don't have to suffer in one area to build in another area. God is El Shaddai, the many-breasted one. That means he's got a breast for all the different areas of life. He has a breast for all of his children to feed in every area of life. He has vacation provision. He has housing provision. He has food provision. You don't have to skimp on food to live in a nice home. You don't have to live in less of a home to go on vacation more. God has provision for every area of life, without another area having to suffer.

"Hey, do you want to go bowling?"

"We can't. We've decided to allot $50 a month for entertainment as a couple. And we've already exhausted that."

You hear people say that because now we're living how others won't, one day we'll live how others are unable to. But I doubt it. Just like you can't put a mask on and decide to be fearful for a year and a half and then switch it off, you can't be cheap for 30 years and then suddenly decide to start spending money. You create thought and life patterns. Jesus didn't operate like that.

I was preaching an extended revival meeting. A man came up to me and said, "I've already put money in your offering, but I wanted to give this to you personally." And he gave me a check for $5,000. I took it. I cashed it.

The people at the bank said, "Can I ask what you will use this money for?"

I said, "I'm going to buy a Barbie for my kid." In other words, mind your own business.

I got the money, went to a jewelry store, and bought my wife a gorgeous ring. I gave it to her, a symbol of my love to which she responded, "Thank you. But I thought we were going to go on vacation." This was back then, and we hadn't been on a vacation ever. She said, "As God started to bless us, I thought we would save up for a vacation."

This must have come out of my spirit because at that time I didn't even know what I'm teaching you right now. I said, "God has ring money and God has vacation money." I could tell she kind of didn't believe me. I told her, "I promise you, before this meeting is over, someone will give me money for a vacation." The next day, another person gave me a check for $7,500, and said the same thing as the other guy, "I already put money in your offering, but this is for you personally." The next day I showed her the check and said, "Told you so." And gave it to her for a vacation.

Let that point get into your spirit, it will help you. You don't have to cheap out on other stuff because you have a noble goal.

"We're not going to go out to eat anymore because I want to save up and get us a house." People who operate like that are not givers. You aren't a God-like giver, directed by the Holy Spirit, if you set aside an amount every month to give, for entertainment, to go to the movies, or whatever. That doesn't work. It doesn't work in the area of giving because the Holy Ghost actually doesn't care how much you've allotted for giving.

The Holy Spirit will test you sometimes. Was Isaac in Abraham's giving budget?

"Give me your son, your only son, Isaac."

"Actually, God, I've set aside $200 a month to give in sacrifices, and I've already exhausted that this month."

No, the Holy Ghost will test you. If you get locked into that little setup of what some call stewardship—I call being a miser—you'll never operate in the financial anointing.

I'm talking about a financial anointing. What's a financial anointing? When I preached at a church that had 130 people, and $1.1 million came in the offering, that's an anointing. You can't make that happen. You can't pressure 130 people to give $1.1 million. That's an inducement from Heaven that brings about supernatural results. That's what I'm teaching. I'm not teaching "20 laws to get rich." I'm teaching "20 laws that govern a financial anointing," where money flows to you en masse, without effort.

Just as there is a financial anointing, there's a healing anointing. Rod Parsley was with Lester Sumrall backstage before they went out to preach. Lester Sumrall put his hand on his stomach and said, "Oral Roberts is in the building."

Rod Parsley said, "No, he's not coming tonight. He never called me. He's coming later in the week." And when they walked out, there was Oral Roberts. Rod said, "How did you know he was here?"

Lester said, "I felt his healing anointing." There's a healing anointing. There's also a salvation anointing, which is why some people are massive soul-winners—it's by the anointing. That anointing is not a mystery; there are laws that govern everything. There are laws that govern the healing anointing, and there are laws that govern the financial anointing.

Now, obviously, the disciplined person who saves money is going to outperform the person who doesn't save anything and doesn't give much. But givers outperform savers. Solomon, the richest man who ever lived, did not acquire his wealth through saving and good fiscal management. He acquired his wealth by giving 1000 burned offerings to the Lord. You know how many he was supposed to give? Seven. And he said, "I'm going to give a thousand."

Solomon set a goal. He believed in God to help him be the king and give him wisdom. He received what he asked for.

REFUSING TO PROVIDE FOR AND BLESS YOUR FAMILY IRRITATES GOD

Refusing to provide for your family invites God's anger. Refusing to bless your family is an irritation to God. And when I say family, I'm talking about nuclear family: wife, children, not your cousin Ray-Ray.

The only problems Abraham really had resulted from bringing his nephew with him. When the Lord told him: *Leave your father's house and your family and go to the land that I'll show you*, he brought one family member with them. That guy was a problem, Lot. What was the other problem? The other lady that lived in their house to help his wife. She was a problem. Keep your home a nest for you, your spouse, and your children. If you feel compelled to help somebody else, get them an apartment. Don't let them live in your kids' bedroom. It's a mistake. You're free to disagree, but I'm right.

My father's a preacher. He helps people for a living. He loves people. He has a great heart for people. My mother has an even bigger heart to help people. They never take people into their home. It's asking for trouble. It's asking for molestation. It's asking for problems. You don't bring outsiders into your home. At the end of the day, you need a place of peace. Jesus didn't do that. Jesus brought his disciples with him on the boat and went somewhere to sleep. He didn't bring the blind people and the lepers on the boat with them. He healed them, gave them instruction, and retreated.

> But those who won't care for their relatives, especially those in their own household, have denied the true faith. Such people are worse than unbelievers.
>
> — 1 TIMOTHY 5:8

Refusing to provide for your family draws the anger of God. Refusing to bless your family is an irritation to God because it's the opposite of his nature. God blesses His family. God said that even evil fathers know how to give good gifts to their children. You should bless your children. You shouldn't shoot down every request they have. I'm not saying to spoil them, but you shouldn't find a way to shoot down every request they have.

"I want to go to Disney."

"We can't afford that."

"I want to go to the beach."

"That's a long way from where we live. You know how much gas is?"

You're wrecking your child. They're never going to become a person who operates in faith. You're taking your limitation and lack of faith and imparting it to your children. Take note of what they want, and when they do something good, bless them. You can do all kinds of things that don't cost any money. We went to the beach a couple of weeks ago for the weekend as a family. When the trip was over, Camila said, "I like going to the beach with you guys, better than I like going to Disney World." The beach is free.

You can spend time together in a different location, go to state parks, or rent a boat. It doesn't have to be stuff that breaks the bank. People are reading this right now who are over 50 years old, and perhaps you and your dad still share an extremely strong bond built around fishing or hunting. So, find whatever works for your child and build a relationship doing it.

It was a big frustration for my father because I didn't enjoy fishing or hunting. My dad didn't have much money starting out, but general admission for Pirates games was just $2 when I was a kid in the 80s. My dad would shell out the $4. He'd take me multiple nights in a week, on school nights. Baseball's a great sport to develop a relationship with somebody because it's boring, long, pretty quiet and you can talk.

I vividly remember going to those games with my dad; it made me happy. Even though we were sitting in the cheapest seats in the third tier, I brought my glove. It would have been something for somebody to hit a 600-foot shot, but I had my glove ready to catch it. After about the fourth inning, the ushers let us come down and sit in the lower seats.

LIFE PRIORITIES ARE IMPORTANT

The priorities in your life are important. These four entities are the top priority of your life, in order.

God, number one.

Spouse, number two.

Children, number three.

Church, number four.

"Well, you think somebody should put their spouse and their children ahead of the kingdom of God and the church?" If your marriage is a mess and your children are a mess, you're not going to be a help to your church. You're a drain on your church. So, if you want to help your church, have a stable family that doesn't need continual prayer. If you're going to help the church, you need a strong marriage and spiritually healthy children.

God, first. Out of that will flow your correct marriage. Spouse, second. Children, third. Church fourth.

By children, I mean raising them in the fear and admonition of the Lord. I don't mean prioritizing your daughter's travel cheer squad and your son's travel baseball team, traveling on Sunday and preventing church because "Jonathan said kids should be ahead of the church."

God, spouse, children, and church. I'm saying that because there's a lot of men and women who use church like marijuana. They use it as an escape from their family. They're not spiritual, they go to church to flee their marriage and to flee their marriage responsibilities. They go to church and don't spend any time with their children. Their spouse and children end up resenting the church. That's not spirituality, it's abandoning your spouse and children to go pray all day. I'm not buying it. I'm telling you as a minister, I don't buy it. Have you ever noticed the ladies that wave flags at church are usually alone? "I have flag recital on Thursday nights and then I'm on the intercessory prayer team." Where's your husband? Why don't you go practice with him a few days a week? You can't shuck your family responsibilities under the guise of the prophetic flag ministry. Just some free advice. Don't use church as an escape from your family.

YOUR NUCLEAR FAMILY TAKES PRIORITY

You are responsible to your nuclear family before your parents and far before your extended family. You have a scriptural mandate to provide for your spouse and your children. You do not have a scriptural mandate to provide for your cousin who needs a place to live. This is another place where people mess their marriages up. You don't let your brother live in your home. Your wife's vacuuming, and he's got his feet up, and she has to ask him to move his feet. It's going to cause problems. He doesn't belong there.

"My mother said that she doesn't want us to go to that church, but my wife wants to go to that church, and I want to go. But how do I rectify that with the Bible saying to honor your father and mother?"

Honoring doesn't mean being raised by them when you're 50-years-old. That's not your mother's place. The Bible says when you get married, *for this reason, does a man leave his father and mother and cling to one wife.* So you honor your parents, but they are not a second voice in your marriage.

"My wife's telling me this, but then my mother…"

Your mother needs to buzz off. She's out of line. Tell her I said so. She needs to mind her own freaking business.

"My mom doesn't think we should live in that neighborhood."

Who asked her? Quit running your decisions by other people. Want to hear a great secret to having peace in life? Let them find out after you did it.

Did Abraham run his decisions by everybody?

"Hey, just so you know, I'm leaving you and my native country. What do you guys think about that?"

They'd have talked him out of it. He didn't even know where he was going. God said, "Go to the land, then I'll show you." He never even told him where he was going.

You are responsible to your nuclear family before your parents and far before your extended family. Certain cultures believe if you are financially blessed, you are expected to take care of your cousins, your uncle, etc., as you rise up in wealth.

I'm going to tell you a saying, that's an old saying in Africa; "If you have one rich person and six poor people, soon you'll have seven poor people." Do you understand that? Because the needs of the six will drain the resources of the one. You can't help everybody, and you never let people manipulate you into helping them. Don't allow yourself to be manipulated.

If someone contacted this ministry, and said, "With all God's blessed you with, it'd be very easy for you to send our ministry a thousand dollars." I'll tell you I not only wouldn't give them anything, I'd look to break something they own. Don't talk like that. I don't owe you anything. When I didn't have any resources, I never contacted anybody privately for help, ever.

A man on our board of directors was the CEO of a bank, a multi-multimillionaire. I never privately contacted him, ever, for money or asked him to please pray that money comes in. Not even creative begging, which many Christians are masters at.

Creative begging. "Does anyone know where we can get a couch?"

Yeah. The couch store.

"Does anyone know where we can get a moving truck?"

Yeah. The moving truck store. Quit trying to disguise your begging as "I have a question." Try typing that exact same phrase into Google instead of Facebook, and it'll tell you the answer to your question. Beggars can never be blessed—never. It's not your clothes that make you a beggar. It's not sitting on the street that makes you a beggar. It's the act of begging that makes you a beggar. Many ministers are well-dressed beggars. Many Christians are decently dressed beggars.

How many celebrities could we talk about who felt a need when they became wealthy to put their cousins on their payroll and let their family bleed them out of money? I'm talking extended family. You don't have a Bible responsibility to your cousins. You don't have a Bible responsibility to your uncles and aunts. That's their children's responsibility. You can bless them. I'm not saying don't help them. I'll tell you this, immediately stop helping anybody who expects it and doesn't appreciate it. Extended family, friends, or whoever.

Be prepared when you help people. A, they're not going to pay you back. And B, they won't just be ungrateful, they're going to resent you for not doing more. So, if you know that upfront, you won't get upset. That's how people are. Don't let it affect you, just know you don't have a responsibility to help. You have a responsibility to take care of your spouse. When's the last time you bought something nice for your spouse?

Relationships are supposed to be reciprocal. Many of us were raised in homes where it seemed like the wife was supposed to do everything, and the husband was supposed to sit and watch TV and wonder why things weren't ready sooner. Don't do that. That is not a recipe for a strong marriage. You lose your wife, you lose your wealth. So, it all ties together. You do have a responsibility to take care of your spouse. Quit complaining and bless them. Quit thinking about what they can do for you and think about what you can do for them. And with that, you do have a responsibility to train up and bless your children.

HONOR YOUR FATHER AND MOTHER

Honor your father and mother. Although your responsibility to your spouse is far above your responsibility to your parents, though your parents should not meddle in your marriage, the Bible does command you to honor your father and mother. And I'm telling you, financially, honor your father and mother. This is the first commandment. There is no honor in the Bible without cost. It's not saying nice things. You do things that matter to honor them. Anybody can run their mouth.

"Dad, I just want you to know, I honor you. And in this church, we have a genuine culture of honor."

Do you? Who have you honored, and how did you honor them?

"This church has a real honor culture." That sounds like something people say instead of giving something of substance.

Honor your father and mother. When's the last time you gave your father or mother a sizeable financial gift or bought them property? Send them on vacation. It's not about the money you have, it's about a mentality. If you understand that it's one of the laws that will help the financial anointing flow to you, then you do things to honor your father and mother.

I sent a private jet to pick up my father when he finished preaching and flew him home. That costs a decent amount of money. I did it to honor him. Am I going to fly myself all over the country and not my dad?

MAKE UP YOUR MIND EARLY

Make up your mind that when the Lord increases your wealth, you're not going to swap your wife out for another wife. There are things you should make up your mind on ahead of time.

Do you know how evil it would be for me to get rid of Adalis and marry somebody else? She came up with me from the time when I had nothing. She was at my side. By the grace of God, she did more to build this ministry than I did. I'm not saying it to be humble. I have never said anything to be humble. How can you go from nothing to something, kick your wife out, and bring someone else in?

Make up your mind that the wife who was your partner when you built what you have is not getting kicked out later in life. I would flip it and say the same to the wives concerning their husbands, but it's more of a husband thing. You don't hear many stories about a wife getting rich and divorcing her husband so she can marry a younger man.

Don't let the Devil bring discontentment into your home. When he does, he's trying to crack the foundation of your life and your wealth. Don't allow yourself to be discontent in your marriage. If you allow discontentment, you'll never stop finding things to be discontent about.

"I don't feel like my wife respects me."

Who cares how you feel? What are you, an emotionally unstable 13-year-old at Hot Topic?

"I don't feel respected."

Well, quit living in your feelings.

If you allow discontentment in your life, you'll never stop finding things to be discontent about. Allow yourself to have a spirit of thankfulness, which exudes from the Holy Ghost. You can always find something to be thankful for.

> Let your wife be a fountain of blessing for you. Rejoice in the wife of your youth. She is a loving deer, a graceful doe. Let her breasts satisfy you always. May you always be captivated by her love.
>
> — PROVERBS 5:18-19

Men, the Bible instructs that the only boobies that should be satisfying you are those of the wife of your youth. *May you be captivated by her love. Why be captivated, my son, by an immoral woman? Or fondle the breasts of a promiscuous woman? For the Lord sees clearly what a man does, examining every path he takes. An evil man is held captive by his own sins; they are ropes that catch and hold him. He will die for lack of self-control; he will be lost because of his great foolishness.*

That's a Bible instruction. You make up your mind that "It's my wife and me until death do us part." That's a principle of wealth creation, and it's a law that governs the financial anointing.

CREATE TRANSGENERATIONAL WEALTH

Create transgenerational wealth like your father, Abraham. A good man leaves an inheritance to his children's children. A righteous man leaves an inheritance to his children's children. Make plans to perpetuate your wealth through your children; they should not have to start where you started. Many of you started at the bottom, but your children don't have to start at the bottom.

If I acquire land and a home for Camila before she leaves my house, and this is how she starts off, that will affect her and her children. That's how to start building wealth through generations.

Think past your life. You should think according to the Bible. A righteous man leaves an inheritance to his children's children. You should start thinking down the line.

For my grandchild, there should be people that hate the kid. "Oh, she's a Shuttlesworth. Everything was given to her." Yes. Correct. Because the kid had a grandfather that started thinking about this at 40, not at 84.

Satan is a master of discontent. I want you to think of this with me. Satan got Eve to be discontent in the Garden of Eden. That's phenomenal. Everything was perfect. There was nothing wrong. Then Satan got Eve to be discontent with one tree from which she couldn't have the fruit. Insane, totally insane.

The Devil, if allowed, can make anybody discontent anywhere. Don't allow it. If you start feeling sorry for yourself, you can be sure it's not God talking to you. The Holy Spirit never says to anybody, "People don't appreciate you like they should." That's the Devil. So you don't entertain those thoughts. It's the beginning of a destroyed garden. They got kicked out of the Garden of Eden because they let the Devil make them discontent in a perfect relationship. Don't let it happen. Slam the door on discontentment.

Since we're talking about honoring your family and honoring your spouse, I want you to think of something small that your spouse likes that you could get for them today. This has nothing to do with being rich. It's a mindset. If you brought me a large hot Dunkin' Donuts' coffee made the way I like it, you couldn't bring me much else to make me happier. So that's a $2.20 thing someone could buy that would bring me joy.

Your husband has something like that. Your wife has something like that. What's her favorite dessert? Get it and bring it home to her. Call it in for pickup. Your wife loves cheesecake from the Cheesecake Factory. Go get one. It's not going to alter your life.

"But it's $40!"

You're probably not going to be 82, sitting on your porch going, "I wish I had the freaking $40 back I spent on that cheesecake." Get her a slice of it. What's your husband's favorite thing to eat? Call it in and bring it home. I'm not talking about the A5 Wagyu steak from the West of New Zealand. I'm talking about him liking hot dogs from Five Guys. Order two. You can do stuff for almost no money that'll make somebody really love you.

It's not the coffee. It's not the hot dogs. It's not the cheesecake. It's that you care. You're showing you care. You're showing you love.

I would go upstairs in my free time to play video games and take a Red Bull and a little bag of Cheetos with me. I was up there playing video games one day, and Camila walked upstairs, carrying a Red Bull and a little bag of Cheetos, and gave me a hug. I'm telling you, from that day forward, I've been thinking about getting her land and a home. Because it's not the thing, it's that you care. How did she, at six years of age, notice exactly what I eat and drink and bring it to me? I'm tearing up thinking about it.

You used to do that for your wife when you were dating. You used to do that for your husband when you were dating. At some point, it stopped. Start it up again. When your husband makes an offhand comment about something he likes, put it on an Amazon watch list, and wait for the price to drop or whatever you have to do to get it. It's not the gift. It's an investment in the relationship.

You're blessed in Jesus' name. Discontentment will never find a resting place in your home in Jesus' name. Your marriage will grow stronger from today in Jesus' name. Your children are blessed. They're going to make you proud in Jesus' name. Amen.

LAW TEN

THE LAW OF JOY

When people are happy, they spend money. When people are sad, they don't spend money. So, for wealth to follow you, either you personally have to produce joy for people, or you have to have a product that gives people joy; this is The Law of Joy.

> But the believers who were scattered preached the
> Good News about Jesus wherever they
> went. Philip, for example, went to the city of
> Samaria and told the people there about the
> Messiah. Crowds listened intently to Philip because
> they were eager to hear his message and see the
> miraculous signs he did. Many evil spirits were
> cast out, screaming as they left their victims. And
> many who had been paralyzed or lame were
> healed. So there was great joy in that city.
>
> — ACTS 8:4-8

If you think this law isn't real, ask yourself why there are people who tell jokes for a living who also own their own planes or fly in private jets. They tell jokes and get paid $40,000 or $80,000 or more for one hour of work. People will pay you to make them happy because joy is a rarity in the world, and it seems to be even rarer with each passing day.

One of the wealthiest ministries on Earth is criticized by religious people. "All he does is tell jokes." They don't get it; people have miserable lives. They have a strained relationship with their spouse, children, or both. Their boss is semi-abusive to them. If you can do something that makes people smile, you won't lack money. People who don't have $200 in the bank will shell out close to $2,000 to have an iPhone because that phone brings them joy—you see people walking around with a slight smile, looking at their phones.

I'm very dogmatic about happy music in my revival meetings—especially if it's a crusade. People have worked a long day by the time they get to my meeting in the evening. Yet, most worship leaders do not understand how to properly do praise and worship for a revival meeting.

It's not Sunday morning church. People have worked from eight o'clock till five o'clock; they're tired. They don't need to come into church, hear sad and slow music, and be sung to sleep. Furthermore, you can't access God's presence without joy.

> Enter his gates with thanksgiving; go into his courts with praise. Give thanks to him and praise his name.
>
> — PSALM 100:4

You cannot enter into God's presence without joy because there's no such thing as sad praise. Praise is an expression of joy, and joy attracts money. Sorrow repels money.

There are people you will pay to listen to for an hour because they make you laugh. Then there are people you might pay to shut up, because after 15 minutes they make you depressed.

It's important to play an upbeat, joyful, strong praise song when people leave a meeting. Your last memory of a place determines whether you'll return. If you just worked all day, sat at church for 2-3 hours, and heard a funeral song on your way out, you're going to stay home the rest of the week. There needs to be joy; the atmosphere and music needs to be happy and upbeat.

My revival meetings are happy meetings. There's laughter throughout the whole meeting. Bishop David Oyedepo said, "If you have any of my preaching recordings and you don't hear me laugh at least once while I'm preaching, throw the recording away." In other words, I'm not in the spirit of God if I don't have joy. The place where you create joy is where you'll create your prosperity.

Where you produce joy, there is the opportunity for you to create wealth. We do a program at night called Check the News. People think they watch it to get news, but they actually watch it to laugh.

Almost every other news show tells you the world's going to end. "We're in trouble. Christians are being hunted down." But on our program, we mock the church's enemies, and people laugh themselves to sleep. They come back and watch almost every night because it produces joy. Joy might be one of the rarest things in the world.

You'll never lack money if you can produce joy for people, either personally or with a product. When's the last time you made someone laugh from their belly, or when's the last time you did something that brought a broad smile to someone's face? Do you bring sorrow where you go, or do you bring joy? It will determine your prosperity.

> And Nehemiah continued, "Go and celebrate with a feast of rich foods and sweet drinks, and share gifts of food with people who have nothing prepared. This is a sacred day before our Lord. Don't be dejected and sad, for the joy of the Lord is your strength!"
>
> — NEHEMIAH 8:10

As you grow in wealth, you have to decide to stay in joy if you're going to keep your enemy from having the upper hand. You will observe the same in any character in the Bible. The enemy doesn't just say, "Well, let them have the money." No, the enemy comes to try to mess with the blessing God's giving you.

You can read that in Genesis 26 very clearly. They deported Isaac. They stopped up his wells. The enemy will buffet you and get you to back down. Suppose the enemy can get you tired and weary. In that case, you'll fail physically and mentally, and you'll stop producing, or there will be a drastic reduction in your prosperity.

The joy of the Lord is your strength. If you stay joyful, you stay in strength. If you stay in strength, you stay in victory. Guard your joy. It's very important.

I keep about five videos queued up on my YouTube page on my phone. Suppose Camila is crying because she fell off her bike, or she ran and tripped and fell. In that case, I can play one of those five videos. She'll immediately go from crying to laughing. With the blood still running down her leg, she's laughing uncontrollably. Joy is a powerful thing.

Make a concerted effort to remove anything from daily life that doesn't bring joy. Joy is a sign that you're in the will of God.

It's not only important to do what you enjoy, it's also important to enjoy the process. Anything you don't enjoy will wear you out over time. It'll shorten your life and shorten your career or ministry.

Guard your joy. Guard your joy ferociously. I remove people from my life that don't bring me joy. Some people dread going to their own business or ministry office because of the sad people there. They avoid their own assignment, so they don't have to be around certain people. That's a problem.

Guard your joy by placing things and people in your daily routine that bring you joy. There's an old saying, "Instead of planning a vacation, build a life that you don't want to take a break from." Most people live in misery and then look forward to one week, where they take a break from the prison they've built for themselves. Make every day such that you enjoy what you do; there's a way to do it.

Put pictures up in your house that bring you joy. What was the best day you ever had in your life? Do you have any pictures from it? Get one blown up big and put it in your house. I would not have a picture in my house of a family member who died tragically. It's not that you don't remember them, but you don't need that image in your field of vision every freaking hour of every day, snapping you out of a good mood.

Foundationally, I don't let anything make me an unhappy person. An unhappy person can't produce joy for other people. If it's a law governing the financial anointing that joy produces wealth, you can't produce joy from an unhappy place.

You should grow in everything that's good and godly, and joy is a fruit of the spirit. You shouldn't have less joy as you get older, you should have more joy as you get older.

When you produce joy, there's an opportunity to produce wealth. In the Old Testament of the Bible, you weren't allowed to appear sad in the king's presence. The king only allowed happy people around him. Solomon had happy people around him as the king. Be happy, keep happy people around you, and produce something that makes people happy. That's what I do in the ministry.

Guard your joy. Be a joyful person. Keep joyful people around you. Produce joy for other people. It's a law that governs the financial anointing.

LAW ELEVEN

THE LAW OF PROTECTION

You're a fool if you don't understand that as you grow in wealth, there are people who will conspire to strip you of your wealth; this is The Law of Protection.

> Then the other administrators and high officers began searching for some fault in the way Daniel was handling government affairs, but they couldn't find anything to criticize or condemn. He was faithful, always responsible, and completely trustworthy. So they concluded, "Our only chance of finding grounds for accusing Daniel will be in connection with the rules of his religion."
>
> — DANIEL 6:4-5

When you hear the word thief, you think of a guy in a black mask and black and white striped shirt, breaking into buildings. There's a higher level of thievery, white-collar theft. Some people will make plans to tie you up in court over unjust charges, who know they'll lose the case. Their aim is to financially drain you through millions of dollars in legal expenses, so the lawyer can give a kickback to the mastermind of the lawsuit.

There are many ways people can steal from you. If you had put $100 in a bank in 1960, that $100 would now be worth $20 compared to what it was worth in 1960. Even a safe can't keep your money protected from the government stealing it through inflation. There are forces at work to strip you of your money, and if you don't honor the law of protection, you'll lose what God gave you.

When we built our television studio, it was outfitted with state-of-the-art equipment. I told Patrick, our administrator, "If this place is ever broken into, and this equipment is vandalized or stolen, you're fired. I want you to plan this office like you know someone will break in and steal it. I want you to put in place systems making it impossible to steal or vandalize."

I want to keep Patrick with me for the rest of my life. I wasn't saying that to threaten him. I wanted him to know I'm not a brain-dead minister who says, "Our church was burned down." Why was your church burned down? It wasn't burned down because there was an arsonist. It was burned down because you were too cheap to pay a security guard $15 an hour to patrol the property. That's why your church was burned down.

What you don't protect, you lose. How many churches have to be burned down before you realize your responsibility is to protect God's house?

I'll tell you another thing I told Patrick. I said, "When I say make sure it can't be vandalized or stolen, I don't just want a videotape of the guy who did it. I don't want to hear, 'We have footage of it.' I want there to be a price paid for attempting to break in."

This is not merely a video screen, video cameras, monitors, and a microphone. This is 20 years of my life that I've worked for. This is the growth of that work. I'm not turning it over to rioters and looters. I'd happily watch them being mauled by a dog before I gave them any piece of equipment.

I've decided to protect what God's put in my hands. I'll protect my wife, my daughter, and my ministry with my life, and I'll protect the people God has entrusted to me in ministry with my life.

Success brings enemies. Let me ask you: What did Daniel ever do to anybody for men to gather and plot against him and be thrown to lions? Some people hate you just because you have what they don't have. They don't care that you worked. They don't care what your purpose is. They don't care about the time you put in. They hate that somebody rose higher than them. It's called jealousy and envy. It's a sin that's a fruit of the Devil, and some people are full of the Devil.

From the opening passage, I want you to notice that before they passed the law, the Bible says they sought a way to find something wrong in how Daniel conducted his affairs. When you start a business or a ministry, some people will make it their life's work to expose fraud and unethical activity.

Was Joseph accused of rape and convicted of rape in the Bible? Yes. Did he ever rape anybody or do anything inappropriate sexually? No. Accusers don't care about facts. Never spend time trying to explain yourself to people committed to misunderstanding you.

People write all kinds of stuff about me. I don't respond. I don't care. They're doing what they've been anointed by the Devil to do; attack, and falsely accuse. They're not interested in truth. Just like the men who plotted against Daniel, their motivation was to take him down, that's it. They didn't want to hear his side of the story. Before they passed a law to prevent Daniel from praying to his God, they first looked at his integrity, ethics, how he handled his finances, or whether he stole money.

There's a preacher I know—he's not a bad guy—who's in federal prison right now serving a multi-year sentence for illegal financial activity.

You must set up your life, business, and ministry as if you know an undercover FBI agent has been assigned to drop accusations and take you down. You need to not only stay away from shady or unethical and illegal activities, but you also need to follow the principle we learned from Joseph.

It's not enough just to maintain innocence; you must be able to prove you haven't done anything wrong. I take two people on the road with me when I travel. If I go out to eat with somebody by myself, that person could say I said or did something wrong. Even though I could deny their accusation, it's my word against theirs. There are plenty of people who already don't like me, who would happily believe my accuser. But, if two people are eating with me and I'm accused of something inappropriate or illegal, I have two witnesses to corroborate my innocence. The other person would have no witnesses. I would not only be able to defend myself, but I would also sue them for defamation. I would sue them as harshly as I could because this is one instance where you don't turn the other cheek. It's important to be able to counter-sue when accusations are made against you because that is proof to the public that the other person is full of crap.

If a lady says that I touched her breast and all I do is deny the allegations, you will believe that something must have taken place.

You might think, "He's just saying it didn't happen, but he's backing off." But, if a lady accuses me of being inappropriate, of sexual harassment, and I say, "Not only are the claims false, I will sue you for $20 million for trying to take me and my ministry down." You have to set things up not only to avoid wrongdoing but also to prove you've never done anything wrong.

The only way you'll go through life avoiding people who want to destroy you is if you are not doing anything to make an impact. If you do things that matter, your business or ministry will increase. There will be people assigned by hell to take you down, and you need to prepare for it from the beginning.

> ...even though I have received such wonderful revelations from God. So to keep me from becoming proud, I was given a thorn in my flesh, a messenger from Satan to torment me and keep me from becoming proud.
> Three different times I begged the Lord to take it away. Each time he said, "My grace is all you need. My power works best in weakness." So now I am glad to boast about my weaknesses, so that the power of Christ can work through me. That's why I take pleasure in my weaknesses, and in the insults, hardships, persecutions, and troubles that I suffer for Christ. For when I am weak, then I am strong.
>
> — 2 CORINTHIANS 12:7-10

Paul wasn't asking to be delivered from sickness when God said: *My grace is sufficient for you.* There was a literal messenger from Satan, a person sent by the Devil to harass him. Well, what do you see happen in the ministry of Paul in the Bible? He's preaching somewhere. Men come and stir up a riot against him, make false claims about what he's saying, and get him thrown in prison. That's what Daniel went through, what Joseph went through, what Jesus went through. Jesus had legal problems, and He didn't do one thing wrong. It's the same with Paul, he had persistent legal issues.

You have to think like the Devil and anticipate how he might take you out. Where is an opening that he can get at? This is why you make sure that all those openings are plugged.

If you have your board of directors set up so they can vote you out of your own ministry, that's a place the Devil can come and attack you. Do you think I'm going to acquire the money to build this property and church and then set the structure of my ministry where the congregation can vote me out? That's a stupid way to operate.

"Our board voted us out of our church."

Why was your board set up so they could vote you out? Who did that? It doesn't have to be set up that way. I'm not going to have anybody from the congregation on our board, it's not scriptural. Sheep don't tell shepherds how to lead.

I have a board of directors. It's made up of ministers who have their own flourishing ministries and some businessmen who have their own flourishing businesses, none of whom desire to be in charge of this ministry. They offer great wisdom and great direction when needed. How can a minister be voted out of his own ministry when his ministry was given to him by God? It can't be taken from him unless he lets it.

I had a friend who I started out in the ministry with. When he went to preach in Canada, I would also preach in Canada with him. He would sell his preaching CDs, and so would I. When he went across the border, they would say, "What's the purpose of your visit to Canada?"

He would say, "I'm visiting friends." But that wasn't why he was going. He was going to preach. That's called a lie.

And then they'd ask, "Are you bringing any goods with you that you intend to leave in Canada?"

"No."

Well, he was. So, he'd hide the CDs inside of clothes in his suitcase.

I made up my mind, if I'm not a cocaine dealer, I'm not going to live like a cocaine dealer. I'm not going to hide Bibles in my clothes to avoid paying a $50 fee.

When I crossed the border, they said, "What's your purpose for coming to Canada?"

"To preach the gospel," I replied.

"At what church?"

A few times they made me pull over and go in for questioning because I'm not coming there to visit friends or family, I'm coming there to do business. Canada didn't seem to like preachers very much. But I'm not lying. I would tell them everything, and it would take longer.

"Are you leaving any goods in Canada?"

"Yes."

"What are you bringing?"

"CDs of my preaching."

I had the form filled out declaring everything I was bringing. And then I paid the money.

My ministry grew, and the other preacher's ministry didn't. Sometimes I wonder if God does not promote someone for their own good.

If you're preaching at a little church in the country out in the woods in Canada, you can tell the border patrol people you're going to visit family. No one knows who you are. You can tell them you're not leaving any goods. You just have a suitcase. But I want to ask you a question... if it was Billy Graham, could he have said, "I'm visiting friends," when coming into Toronto? They would have said, "No, you're not, you're Billy Graham. I've been watching your commercials for over a month. You're lying."

You can lie and run your business dishonestly when you're small. The IRS isn't going to come after you and your business that makes $12,000 a year. It's not worth their time. But if you start bringing in $3.1 million a year, now it's worth their time to look into how you handle your money and your affairs because if you've lied or filled out paperwork falsely, somebody's going to get a payday for catching you.

Deciding to not operate in integrity is deciding to stay small because God won't promote you for your own good.

Some ministers might be praying, "Lord, use me to impact this nation." And God's saying, "If I raised you to that level, you would be in jail by the end of the year." You take money for lunch out of the offering before it's counted. You can do that with your little $300 offering. But suppose you start filling auditoriums, and you start dipping into the money before it's counted. Some people hate the Gospel and would love to see a preacher thrown into a den of lions.

They'd be happy. There are people on assignment from hell to steal what you have and take you down. It's your job to make sure it doesn't happen.

Prayer is never a substitute for wisdom. When I defied the COVID restrictions in our state and held a massive Easter service, I had already consulted one of the best lawyers. I knew someone would call the police during our meeting, so I went ahead and called the police first and paid to have four of them at the meeting. Then, when someone called the police to report our meeting during a public health emergency, the police said, "We're already there, there's nothing wrong." Use your brain. God gave you a brain so you could give Him a break.

Protect your life. I'm not talking about seat belts. If somebody wants to sue you, what safeguards do you have to make it very hard for them? Satan never attacks strength, Satan attacks weakness. If you allow weakness in an area, that's where the Devil will attack. Satan doesn't attack fortified things, Satan attacks things that are open for attack.

The first time there was a church shooting in America, it was tragic. Now, if there's a church shooting, it didn't happen because there was a church shooter; it happened because the pastor is a negligent moron.

It's easy to walk into a church with 40 people and shoot the whole place. But that can't happen at Joel Osteen's church. I could name many other churches just as safe. Do you think the big churches have security because they're big? Or do you think God gave them a lot of people to steward because they honored the law of protection from the beginning?

When God puts people into your care, you protect them. Didn't Jesus teach that there are shepherds, sheep, and wolves who come in to harm the flock? A shepherd deals with wolves. How do wolves manifest? They appear as church shooters and child abusers or molesters. Should a single guy with greasy hair and dirty clothes be allowed to roam around in the lobby by the children's department? No. You tell him to sit down in the service. I'm not allowing some lunatic-looking person to roam around and just wait to see what happens.

Political correctness can get you killed.

"Well, that guy looks like a child molester, but we don't want to judge by the outward appearance. He was behaving weirdly and always hanging around the children's bathrooms. But you know, you don't want to judge a book by its cover."

No. Judging will help you a lot in life. It can keep you alive.

If you don't have a discerning spirit, at least play the odds. Somebody that has an unclean spirit usually has an unclean appearance. If they're acting weird, something's up. Don't wait till it manifests and the problem happens. I watched an episode of forensic files where a young girl was kidnapped, raped, and murdered. Do you know where she was kidnapped from? A Lutheran church. By a guy that would often come in off the street and roam around in the lobby.

I don't know why most churches have ushers. Somebody could walk in and shoot the place up, and they'd hand them a visitor's card. They don't have any foresight, they're just there. They let everybody walk in and out without question. Very few churches have well-trained ushers. Even ones that think they do, somebody can still just run straight down the aisle at the preacher.

At Dr. Rodney's church, once you get to the sixth row from the front, there's a barrier, and an usher has to let you past. They vet you; they take a look at you first. You can't just run up to the front.

How many viral videos have you seen of a preacher and a random guy runs up on the stage and starts yelling at him? How in the world was that guy able to make it to the stage? It's a problem. Christians can be some of the most clueless people on planet Earth.

So how do wolves come in? There are shooters and molesters, then you have what the Bible calls swindlers.

People are probably reading this who went to a church where somebody got members of that congregation involved in some type of financial investment scheme and the swindler ran off with the money. I know of a guy that took about $10 million from the members of a church. That's a wolf. You have murderous wolves, you have sexually immoral wolves, and you have financial wolves. It's a pastor's job to protect the congregation from those kinds of people.

I asked Patrick, who handles finances for our ministry, "What safeguards are in place to prevent an employee from stealing our money." To steal $1 of money from Revival Today, you would have to get my wife in on it, my wife's twin sister in on it, and Patrick in on it. At that point, if my wife turned against me, my ministry is over anyway. When we count the offerings, we don't have the same two people count the offerings each time.

One of my requirements, when I go to speak at a church, is that they allow us to use our own offering envelopes, mostly because I don't trust people to count money who I don't know. One church we went to, my team showed me the offering envelopes, and all the envelopes had been opened. I immediately called the pastor. I was not happy.

I said, "We got our offering envelopes tonight, and they've all been opened."

"Well, I had my people count it before I handed it over to you because we like to give a report to our denomination about what we give to ministries."

I said, "Those envelopes are not yours to touch. That was wrong. I never gave permission for anybody in your church to look in the offering envelopes and count them."

"Well, they're people that I trust."

I said, "They're not people I trust. I don't even know who they are. Do you have a video camera in your counting room?"

"Well, no."

"How many people did you have count?"

"Two."

"Are they the same two people that count every offering?"

"Yeah."

"Okay. You're basically asking to get money stolen."

Do you know who else doesn't touch the offering envelopes? Me. We put them in a hermetically sealed bag. Then they're counted in a room with a video camera, using a rotation of people. If you only have two people count your offerings, then one thief only has to get one other person in on it. If you have a rotation of eight people, with three counting, and they rotate every time, then you have to get eight or nine people to agree on stealing, which is very difficult to do.

People don't use their brains. That's why they are stolen from. God's not going to dump resources into someone that allows thieves to take it. Trustworthy and faithful servants protect what their master gives them. But who is a trustworthy servant? Who is a faithful servant?

You have to operate like this, deciding not to become bitter or paranoid. There will always be some risks, but you manage the risk. If you don't trust anybody, then you just end up firing people left and right.

"They could all turn on you." Yeah, they could. Put systems in place to catch theft or devise a system where the money can't just disappear. Then, still treat people with love. It takes Godly wisdom to do this, but you can do it.

LAW TWELVE

THE LAW OF DEBT REFUSAL

You must first develop a hatred for debt if you're ever going to walk in financial abundance... not *try* to live debt-free, but develop a hatred for borrowing and debt. What I just said is very difficult to process for a Western mind. This is The Law of Debt Refusal. The more educated you are, the harder this will be to process.

> "The Lord will give you prosperity in the land he swore to your ancestors to give you, blessing you with many children, numerous livestock, and abundant crops. The Lord will send rain at the proper time from his rich treasury in the heavens and will bless all the work you do. You will lend to many nations, but you will never need to borrow from them. If you listen to these commands of the Lord your God that I am giving you today, and if you carefully obey them, the Lord will make you

> the head and not the tail, and you will always be on top and never at the bottom."
>
> — DEUTERONOMY 28:11-13

Look how many Bible colleges are, in essence, government-controlled because they receive federal accreditation for student loans. These schools had to close their campuses when told to do so. They had to mask up for COVID. They have to do whatever the government says because they're taking money from the government. *The borrower is servant to the lender.*

There's a pastor of a major church who was diagnosed with cancer. He didn't want to take chemotherapy. He wanted to do natural treatments and believe in God. But because he was the key man on the insurance and the key man on the mortgage to the church, the bank dictated his course of medical treatments and forced him to take chemotherapy.

When the Bible says: *The borrower is servant to the lender*, it means if you borrow money, you are a slave to whoever you borrow money from. They dictate your life. It's a wicked system that God doesn't want you part of.

You have to see debt as wicked. You have to hate it. You'll never get delivered from something that doesn't disgust you. Remember that.

"Well, no, I don't believe we have to take loans. I believe God can provide. But I don't think there's anything wrong with borrowing."

Okay, then enjoy yourself. You're not going to have supernatural stories.

BORROWING IS NOT A SIN, BUT A WEIGHT

The Bible says to *cast off every weight that can easily beset you*. Debt is not an aid in life, debt is a weight. It's not something that helps you, it's something that helps the person who's lending to you. It's not a sin to borrow; there'd only be about six people going to heaven if it was. Borrowing is a weight, and the Bible says to *cast off every weight that will easily beset (persistently trouble) you.*

BORROWING IS ANTI-COVENANT

Abraham didn't borrow. Isaac didn't borrow. Jacob didn't borrow. Then God made it a law in Deuteronomy 28: *If you follow me, you'll lend only, but thou shalt not borrow.* And in Deuteronomy 15:6, *The Lord, your God, will bless you as he has promised. You will lend money to many nations, but you will never need to borrow. You will rule many nations, but they'll never rule over you.* Borrowing is the exact opposite of what God provided for us in the covenant.

This will be difficult for a Western person to latch on to because everything in Western culture is built on debt. The only financial advice I ever received through my 20s from Christians was to be sure to get a good credit score.

"You actually don't want to pay all your bills because then your credit's too good, and people don't want to lend money to you. So, you want to be a little delinquent, leave a little bit of a balance. You want to stay a little bit in debt and be a little bit of a slave because you can borrow more money."

Everything in the West is built on borrowing and debt. It's how the central banks want it, and it's how those in charge want it. They want nations in debt; they want to control nations because they're in debt and they need more money. God said if a nation did what they were supposed to do, that nation would only lend money to other nations. They would never have to borrow money from anybody. As America turned its back on God, debt skyrocketed out of control in proportion to the sin allowed. The national debt is going towards $32 trillion at the writing of this book.

Many of you are reading from nations where your president or prime minister is not actually in charge of that nation; the International Monetary Fund is in charge of your nation. Your leader has to do what he's told, or he's taken out.

Borrowing and debt are not God's intended system for you and me. You're not going to find it in the Bible. In fact, in the Bible, you're actually going to find condemnation of any organization that lends money and charges interest. Historically, Jewish people ended up taking care of the banking in European countries because Christians would not get involved. After all, the Bible condemns it in the Book of Proverbs.

You are not to lend money and charge interest. If a man asks you for your shoes, give him your coat as well. You just give. Either you see borrowing as anti-covenant, or you're always going to have a taste for it.

"Well, we're in an apartment. I'd really like a house. Obviously, I can't save up $450,000, so if I can just get $80,000 as a down payment, the bank said they'll give me money at an interest rate."

And off you go, down the path of debt. Again, not saying it's a sin, but this isn't a book about proper money management; we're talking about 20 laws that govern the financial anointing.

If you're going to walk in the financial anointing, you need a hatred for borrowing, a disgust in your stomach for having your hand out, and for needing someone to give you money.

It doesn't make any sense to my natural mind, but God said it, so I believe it. And if God said it, I believe he's made power available to walk in it. If you see in the Bible that borrowing is anti-covenant and that God made a way to get where you're going without needing financing from mortal man, that will be your first step to getting on a different path.

We're talking about the financial anointing that makes a jar of meal (supposed to last for one lunch) last years; a cruse of oil never run out. These are not laws governing proper money management, these are laws governing the financial anointing.

There is an anointing for money. When you walk outside the financial anointing, you say things like, "How could somebody ever get to a place where they can operate in this life and not need loans?"

What does a loan require? A need. The first thing they're going to ask when applying for a loan is, "What is this for?"

"Well, we would like to buy this property. I'd like to buy this house. I'd like to buy this car."

There's something that you need or require that you don't have the money for, otherwise there's no loan necessary.

"I actually have everything I need, but I just want you to loan me some money." Saying that implies you belong in a mental institution. Borrowing requires a need, and God promised to supply all your needs. So, explain to me, scripturally, how a loan is ever necessary.

You can walk a higher path in the area of finances. You're never going to walk that path if you don't have a hatred for the other path.

As a minister, it's antithetical to everything I am and everything I believe to sit in a cubicle, and ask a heathen banker for money to do what God called me to do. I feel the same about that as I do about sitting in a strip club; I don't belong there.

You put the mortgage officer in a superior position to God because you obviously think God couldn't do what you needed. On the flip side, when you begin to operate above their level, you force people to admit that there must be a God.

GOD PROMISED TO FILL YOUR STOREHOUSES WITH GRAIN

What does that mean? Many faith preachers I know, if they need $300,000 for an event or a crusade, they believe for the money to come in for that crusade. It comes in by the end of the crusade, then they praise the Lord. They were able to pay the $300,000. It all came in the offerings or from partners. Then they have the next event, that's another $300,000, and they need it again. They're always playing from behind. People think playing from behind is normal.

My grandfather was a preacher and had a great disgust for poverty. When my Uncle Ted first started in the ministry, my grandfather drove his car when he came home to make sure everything was working okay.

One day my grandfather said, "Ted, how come every time I drive your car, the fuel level is empty."

My uncle Ted confidently replied, "Because I'm a faith preacher."

My grandfather replied, "It takes more faith to keep it on F than on E."

Faith doesn't play from behind; faith plays from ahead. Faith has an overflowing cup, not an empty cup believing for water.

Don't use faith as a synonym for poverty. "Well, we don't have much because we live by faith." Well, then it's a different faith you're living by than Abraham's faith. Abraham lived by faith and was very rich in livestock, silver, and gold. It takes more faith to live on F than it does on E.

The great American pastor, John Osteen, said you don't have to live off the bottom of the barrel. You can live off the top of the barrel, and you only have to fill the barrel once. Before any need arises, the provision will always be there ahead of time.

I was privileged to be around two different older men of God who were successful pastors and built great churches. In their 80s, both men told me the same thing without knowing each other. They said, "Get to the point in your ministry where you can treat a million dollars like it's zero." What did they mean by that? Don't feel like you've run out of money when you've run out of money. Rather, feel like you've run out of money when you get down to your last million dollars. That's a storehouse principle. Most people will get to zero and then borrow money.

The one pastor, whose church seated about 3,500 people, explained it this way, "If one roof panel fails on my building, it costs $400,000 to replace. So, if that's not in reserve, then I would have to raise the money for it from the pulpit, which will turn off several hundred people who'll leave and go find another church. But if I have no less than a million dollars at my command at any time, when a roof panel fails, we just buy a new one." That's called your storehouse being filled. That's what real faith is.

Real faith doesn't meet the need. Real faith fills your storehouse, so you never have to play from behind. I have never been in a live meeting or on a broadcast and said something like, "Listen, we have a great need. We had some unexpected things come up." If unexpected things happen, it's because you're not an intelligent person. You should expect certain things. Brakes will go. Tires need to be replaced. Roofs need to be fixed. The siding on buildings needs replaced. Cameras wear out. Monitors wear out. Wires stop working. If you run everything with just enough to meet that month's bills, any extra thing immediately becomes an emergency where you need a miracle.

I'm not looking to down-talk anybody, but it's ridiculous to always be in need when God promised to fill your storehouses. You don't have to play from behind. You can play from ahead. You don't have to live off the bottom of the barrel, you can live off the top of the barrel, and you only have to fill the barrel one time. Those two men told me, at 34 years old, that I needed to treat a million dollars as zero.

Looking back on it, there's comfort in the fact that they shared this advice because they saw something in me. They believed I would be at that level one day, even though I was treating zero as zero at the time. There was no option to treat a million dollars as zero because there was no million dollars.

Their words came to pass a few years later, and now we do that. And that way, no financial thing ever becomes something that needs prayer. You can pray about important things like souls, open doors, and spreading the gospel.

If the building needs a new roof, you just buy it. If you need machinery to build a building, you buy it. Play from ahead. Don't wait till the money's run out.

WHEN YOU LEAN ON FLESH, YOU TURN FROM GOD

> This is what the Lord says: "Cursed are those who put their trust in mere humans, who rely on human strength and turn their hearts away from the Lord. They are like stunted shrubs in the desert, with no hope for the future. They will live in the barren wilderness, in an uninhabited salty land.
> "But blessed are those who trust in the Lord and have made the Lord their hope and confidence. They are like trees planted along a riverbank, with roots that reach deep into the water. Such trees are not bothered by the heat or worried by long months of drought. Their leaves stay green, and they never stop producing fruit."
>
> — JEREMIAH 17:5-8

When you learn to receive your healing and physical protection from God, it turns your heart to the scriptures. When you talk to healthy people who've learned to draw their physical strength from God, they talk about the Bible. They talk about healing scriptures. They talk about what they were meditating on from God's Word. When you talk to people who receive their health and strength from the pharmaceutical industry, herbs, or supplements, they talk to you about herbs and supplements. They talk about their medical insurance, or about a specialist they found who does a great job.

When you lean on flesh, you turn your heart away from God. When you meet people who draw their financing from their faith, they talk about the Word. They talk about how great God is. When you meet people who get their financing from the world, they talk about the bank, about credit scores.

"God's given us great favor with our local bank. They gave us a 4.5% rate instead of a 7% interest rate." Bragging about how much money you're having stolen from you is anti-scriptural.

When a church gets paid off, burns the mortgage, and celebrates, the only person who truly should celebrate is the bank. You bought a $1 million building and, over 30 years, paid about $2.5 million for it. God has a better way.

You have two eyes in your head. Can you make one eye look up at the sky and one eye look down at the ground simultaneously? Try it. It hurts. You can't do it. God told Bishop David Oyedepo, "Then neither when you're claiming to look to me, look to man." You have to make up your mind who your source is going to be, man or God.

You have pastors call a congregation member on the stage and say, "If it wasn't for brother Williams, I don't know how this church would survive." And God's up in heaven saying, "Then you and brother Williams can figure out what you'll do. I guess you don't need me anymore." This shows that their trust is in man.

We have a strong 'thank you' system in our ministry. I strongly believe in thanking people and letting them know that I don't take what they've done for granted. But you've never heard me say, "What we're doing is made possible by our partners." Nope. That's reserved for God. "Partners, without you, our ministry wouldn't be able to do what we're doing." Nope. Without God, our ministry wouldn't be able to do what we're doing. God's the reason I have partners. God gets all the glory.

This week, I'm getting an apartment for a young lady in another part of the country because her father beat her. She's in her early 20s. She messaged me and let me know what happened, and just asked me to pray. She wasn't dropping hints. She meant pray, because "I don't have enough for an apartment right now, and I live at home. But this is the second time he's beat me." So, I got her an apartment for a year. She never asked for one. If she asked for one, I probably would let her fend for herself. Begging turns me off. Requesting favors decreases a person's desire to show you any favor.

I met Jesse Duplantis a few months ago. What if I said, "Brother Jesse, do you think I could use your plane sometimes when I go preach if you're not using it?" He never offered. If I ask, he might let me, but he'd never feel like doing anything for me. Begging is a bad way to operate.

In Proverbs, the Bible tells you not to eat the delicacies put before you when you eat with a ruler. Have some class. Some people have class, other people can't spell it. Nobody owes you anything.

IF GOD CAN'T TAKE ME THERE, I DON'T WANT TO GO

For this last part, I am quoting Bishop David Oyedepo. I want you to say these things out loud, and I want you to live by them:

"If God can't take me there, I don't want to go."

"If God can't give it to me, may I never have it."

I'm not trying to get anything. I didn't try to get a ministry office, our ministry grew to the place where it needed an office, and the Lord gave us one. I didn't have a goal of building a church. The Lord spoke to me to do it, and the Lord made it happen. If God can't give it to me, I don't want it. I'm not trying to get things that don't belong to me. I'm not lusting after material things. I'm not trying to acquire anything. If God can't take me there, I don't want to go. I'm not trying to become the top minister in my own strength or have a bigger crusade than another minister my age. That's where you start getting into debt. It's His work. I don't have anything to prove. If God can't do it, then it can stay undone.

The Bible tells you in Psalm 127: *Unless the Lord builds the house, they that labor, labor in vain.* If you do things right, you never have to build anything for God. You'll watch God build for you. If you have to force it, it's not God. If it feels difficult, something's wrong. Godliness with contentment is great gain. That's where the contentment comes in. I'm being fruitful, I'm multiplying, I'm increasing. But I'm not striving. I'm not trying to do anything beyond what God's given me in my assignment to do.

LAW THIRTEEN

THE LAW OF HOLINESS

Holiness is the state or character of being holy or sinless, purity of moral character, perfect freedom from all evil, and sanctified; this is The Law of Holiness.

> If thou return to the Almighty, thou shalt be built up,
>   thou shalt put away iniquity far from thy
>   tabernacles.
>
> — JOB 22:23 (KJV)

> Oh, the joys of those who do not follow the advice of
>   the wicked, or stand around with sinners, or join in
>   with mockers. But they delight in the law of
>   the Lord, meditating on it day and night. They are
>   like trees planted along the riverbank, bearing fruit
>   each season. Their leaves never wither, and they
>   prosper in all they do.
>
> — PSALM 1:1-3

About 80% of you have been taught that you can't be holy or sinless. But in Hebrews 10:14, the Bible clearly teaches that the blood of Jesus cleansed us of all sin and made us holy and without fault. Romans 6:1-14 tells you that not only have you been cleansed of sin and that sin is dead, but you should reckon or consider yourself dead to sin and able to live for the glory of God, and that sin does not have dominion over you.

It is paramount to realize that you can be holy. Holiness isn't a nicety; holiness is a command. Without holiness, no man shall see God. 1 Peter 1:16, *Be ye holy, even as I am holy.* Matthew 5, *Be ye perfect, even as your father in heaven is perfect.* Perfect there does not mean maturity, it means perfect. You can't do that in your own strength, but you can do it in God's strength that He has provided. You must be holy. You must reject the modern church belief that says, "We all sin, don't judge me because I sin differently than you." If you make sin a practice and a lifestyle, you'll go to Hell. Not only will you go to Hell, sin opens the door to the Devil.

If I engage in adultery, the Devil has a way to take my wealth; I can be blackmailed.

"Reverend Shuttlesworth, if you don't pay us $300,000, we'll go to the news and the media and tell them you had sex with this woman, and she can prove it."

Now the Devil has a way to manipulate me. If I have uncontrolled anger, the Devil can exploit that to get me in prison, and it's hard to make money in prison. Therefore, in slamming the door on sin, you slam the door on the Devil's ability to touch your wealth. Sin will destroy your life, and sin will destroy your wealth.

Jesus said: *The prince of this world (talking about Satan) is coming for me. But he can't have me because he has nothing in me.* If you don't allow Satan to infect you with sin, he has nothing in you and has no access to you. But if you compromise and engage on his terms, now he has an open door to mess up your life. Holiness is the master key to a world of exploits. Holiness is the master key; it opens every door in the house.

Deciding to live holy, to live a godly life free from sin, makes your life a magnet for supernatural financial signs and wonders. Sin repels the blessing. Holiness attracts the blessing.

"I mean, God doesn't expect you not to drink any alcohol."

He did for John the Baptist. He did for Samson.

"God never said don't drink, He just said don't get drunk."

John the Baptist and Samson disagree. God told them, *don't ever let strong drink touch your lips.* These two men were set apart to be used mightily of God. So, if your goal is not to go to Hell, that's one thing. If your goal's to be used mightily of God, there's a different set of rules.

Who I stand with matters, the company I keep determines what accompanies me in life. You hang out with adulterers; eventually, you'll commit adultery. You hang out with drunks; eventually, you'll become one. Those that walk with the wise become wise themselves.

The companion of fools will be destroyed. Choosing to associate with fools is a choice to destroy your own life. There are people I could get in a car with on a Friday night, and without me doing one thing wrong, I would still end up in jail. If they decided to do a drive-by shooting with me in the car, no one cares that I'm unarmed. Don't stand around with sinners, and don't join in with mockers. Unbelief is a sin. You can't be blessed like that.

You can join mockers that talk one way, or you can set yourself against them and mock mockers, which I've become very good at.

Here's your secrets to holiness; you guard whose advice you follow, who you stand with, who you join in with or sit with, and you delight in the law of the Lord. You meditate on it day and night. The Word cleanses you. How can a man live holy? Ingest the word of God. God's word cleanses you from the inside out on its own.

> But they delight in the law of the Lord, meditating on it day and night.
>
> — PSALM 1:2

A specific blessing of living holy is bearing fruit in every season. You're also going to have to reject modern church teaching, which says there will be lows and dry seasons. If you expect dry seasons, if you speak dry seasons, you'll have them. But the Bible says righteous men will bear fruit in every season. You will go from glory to glory, victory to victory, and strength to strength.

The time of COVID lockdowns was a dry season for the world. Yet, I heard one Christian after another testify that there was no dry season; instead, it was their best year ever. Even with every external circumstance set up for them to fail.

The Bible says there are no dry seasons for the child of God. Check up on the people who say they're in a dry season, 30 years later they're still in a dry season because they're ignorant of what God clearly said.

The last dry season you went through will be the last dry season you ever have. Every month will be an improvement over the month before. That's what it means to be a tree planted by the water. The Bible says: *Even in famine, they will have plenty.* That means regardless of a stock market crash, real estate market crash, or war, you will have plenty. Natural things can't override the supernatural law that you're tapped into.

When the Lord begins to prosper you, people make it their business to take you out, but God will never allow any work of the enemy to wither the leaves of the righteous man. The things that desire to kill your tree, God will never let them near your tree. He's a hedge of protection. The shield of faith quenches all the fiery darts of the Devil. This includes people who want to cause you legal trouble, people who want to frivolously sue your ministry or business, and people in government who want to shut down your business or ministry, God will go to war against their plan. *Your enemy will come at you from one direction, but I will make him run from you in seven directions.*

We have no record of Daniel praying for God to close the mouth of the lion. God just sent an angel and did it. We have no record of Daniel cursing the men that plotted against him. But God had them and their families fed to the lions in Daniel's place anyway. God defends you for free when you live holy. If you live holy, God defends you without you asking.

The last successful attack against your life, ministry, business, or family will be the last one you ever see in Jesus' name! How would you plan the remainder of this year if you really believed that whatever you touch will only go up?

Father, as we decide to obey and serve you, we thank you for your word that doesn't tell us "some of our days" will have prosperity. We thank you that it tells us all our days will be spent in prosperity.

"If they listen and obey God, they will be blessed with prosperity throughout their lives. All their years will be pleasant."

— JOB 36:11

LAW FOURTEEN

THE LAW OF LOVE AND HONOR

Your prosperity is directly tied to your heart for God's kingdom and your heart for God's servants; this is The Law of Love and Honor.

> Solomon loved the Lord and followed all the decrees of his father, David, except that Solomon, too, offered sacrifices and burned incense at the local places of worship. The most important of these places of worship was at Gibeon, so the king went there and sacrificed 1,000 burnt offerings. That night the Lord appeared to Solomon in a dream, and God said, "What do you want? Ask, and I will give it to you!"
>
> — 1 KINGS 3:3-5

I want you to notice the connection here. He didn't just go and offer a thousand burnt offerings. Solomon so loved the Lord that he gave

1000 burnt offerings. The amount he was supposed to give was seven, and he gave one thousand. I call that extravagant giving. For whatever reason, that part was either left out when I was going to Sunday school growing up, or I just didn't notice it. I always thought God just sovereignly chose Solomon to be super-rich, but, if you read it, like everything else in the Bible, it was provoked.

The gifts of God are free, but they are provoked. Just like when your child does something that touches your heart, and you give them a gift, they don't have to pay for it. You could say the gift they received was free. Though it was free, it wasn't random. It was provoked. There was an action taken that moved you to do something for them, and you're going to see that principle throughout the Bible.

> Then King David turned to the entire assembly and said, "My son Solomon, whom God has clearly chosen as the next king of Israel, is still young and inexperienced. The work ahead of him is enormous, for the Temple he will build is not for mere mortals—it is for the Lord God himself! Using every resource at my command, I have gathered as much as I could for building the Temple of my God. Now there is enough gold, silver, bronze, iron, and wood, as well as great quantities of onyx, other precious stones, costly jewels, and all kinds of fine stone and marble.
> "And now, because of my devotion to the Temple of my God, I am giving all of my own private treasures of gold and silver to help in the construction. This is in addition to the building materials I have already collected for his holy

> Temple. I am donating more than 112 tons of gold from Ophir and 262 tons of refined silver to be used for overlaying the walls of the buildings and for the other gold and silver work to be done by the craftsmen. Now then, who will follow my example and give offerings to the Lord today?"
>
> — 1 CHRONICLES 29:1-5

Why did David give? Because of his affection for the Temple of the Lord. You should just keep anything you give that isn't provoked by love for God's kingdom. If you pay your tithes like a tax, it will not work well. There's no affection if you give offerings because somebody cheered it out of you. If you say, "You know what, that was a good revelation. I've never heard that before, I'm going to give some money," there's no affection. Give because of your heart for God, your heart for God's house, your heart for God's servants.

David collected materials from all his allies and other countries, but he emptied his own private treasury into it. Many preachers are experts at collecting other people's money, but they don't give anything themselves. "We, as a church, gave $200,000 to missions." Yeah. The people in your church gave that. How much of that did you give? Because the people in your church will be blessed, your church will be blessed, but what about you?

David didn't just say, "Look at everything I collected from these other people." He said, "Here's everything I collected from others, and now I'm emptying my own private treasury into the Temple. I am donating 112 tons of gold." Today this would be worth about $6.1 billion. Just David's gold offering to the temple alone was $6.1 billion, not counting the silver. The silver was 262 tons of silver. This was about a

$10 billion offering for the temple. Why? David said, "Because of my affection for the Lord."

Since the Bible says *don't let your left hand know what your right hand's doing when you're giving*, was David out of line to say this? Well, if he was, why would the Holy Ghost have recorded it in scripture? When the Bible talks about not letting your left hand know what your right hand's doing—if you read it in context—it's about giving to the poor.

You will never see Revival Today point a camera at someone and say, "This is Elaine. She was going to be evicted from her apartment because she's very poor. She's an abuse victim. But we at Revival Today gave her money so she could keep her apartment. And now she's going to tell you how thankful she is." That's embarrassing somebody. The Bible says *when you give to the poor, do it in secret.* Preserve their dignity. In contrast, when you're giving to the work of the Lord, there is nothing wrong with a leader letting people know that he's leading the way in his giving and then challenging the people as David did.

> One day Elisha went to the town of Shunem. A wealthy woman lived there, and she urged him to come to her home for a meal. After that, whenever he passed that way, he would stop there for something to eat.
> She said to her husband, "I am sure this man who stops in from time to time is a holy man of God. Let's build a small room for him on the roof and furnish it with a bed, a table, a chair, and a lamp. Then he will have a place to stay whenever he comes by."
>
> — 2 KINGS 4:8-10

Most Christians are entirely unmoved by what God is moved by. How many people did Elisha pass by in his ministry who said, "Good luck, Elisha. All the best, you're great. We love you." But this lady said, "I can tell this guy's a man of God. I want to make sure he has a place to stay."

> As you know, you Philippians were the only ones who gave me financial help when I first brought you the Good News and then traveled on from Macedonia. No other church did this. Even when I was in Thessalonica you sent help more than once. I don't say this because I want a gift from you. Rather, I want you to receive a reward for your kindness.
> At the moment I have all I need—and more! I am generously supplied with the gifts you sent me with Epaphroditus. They are a sweet-smelling sacrifice that is acceptable and pleasing to God. And this same God who takes care of me will supply all your needs from his glorious riches, which have been given to us in Christ Jesus.
>
> — PHILIPPIANS 4:15-19

I want you to see the parallel between the Shunammite woman in 2 Kings 4 and the Philippian church in Philippians 4. Have you read of any other people, besides the Shunammite woman, who cared where Elisha stayed? "What is he eating? Where does he have to study? We'll furnish his room with a table, a chair, a lamp, and a bed. We'll build an addition onto our home with a private entrance, so he has a place to stay when he travels through."

From the time she did that, the woman received four major blessings. Number one, it provoked the power of God to give her a son. That kind of mindset gave her what money can't buy.

Number two, when the son died, the power of God brought her son back.

Number three, that blessing put a stop to losses. In 2 Kings 8, she received a heads-up about an incoming famine. The Lord kept her ahead of the curve because your losses are God's losses when your money is tied in with the kingdom. So, God will give you a heads-up economically to keep you in the black and out of lack.

Number four, when she came back from having to leave her property, the power of God went to work and restored everything she had lost.

What about the Philippians? Paul was having city-shaking meetings and only one group of people, the Philippians, cared enough to give substantially. They said, "We're not only going to give to you while you're here, we're going to continually send gifts to aid in what God's called you to do." The difference between men is found in their choices.

I started to help older women financially—widows, whose husbands had been in the ministry. I started to honor men of God, who are now coming into the twilight of their life, with monetary gifts. I don't think an 80-year-old guy should have to preach every week to make sure he has a place to live. Somebody should help him. Someone should take action like the Shunammite woman felt about Elisha. When I started helping people in this way, our ministry began commanding more wealth than it ever did before.

I have a friend with a wealthy ministry. I found out he has paid for countless preachers' widows' homes and pays for their 24-hour nursing care. The financial increase has exploded for his ministry.

He who receives a prophet in the name of a prophet shall receive a prophet's reward. What does that mean? How did they receive Jesus in His hometown? "Oh, this is Jesus; we know His brothers." They didn't give Him any honor; to them, He was Jesus, the son of Joseph. But to other people, like the lady that poured the alabaster box on His feet, He wasn't just the son of Joseph; He was Jesus the Christ, the anointed one, the Messiah.

Sometimes Christians, who have been saved a long time, get a cavalier attitude towards ministers. Even ministers can gain a cavalier attitude towards other ministers. "Well, that's our pastor, Jim. We just call him Jim. We voted out our last pastor, and then a couple guys sent in resumes. We decided to vote in Jim."

To them, he is just Jim. But to other people, he's a gift from God, who God's hand is upon, not a regular person. When you recognize that, and you make up your mind that you're going to financially honor this person, it is what the Shunammite woman did. It's what the Philippian church did.

God doesn't have to reduce another ministry to bless my ministry. And if another ministry is blessed through my ministry, it will never reduce my ministry. God doesn't have to take something off a person's plate to put it on somebody else's plate. He's El Shaddai, the God of more than enough.

Honoring someone is not calling them onto the platform and letting everyone know you honor them. That's not it—that's just words. Financial honor is what the Shunammite woman did. That's what the Philippian church did. That's what the woman with the alabaster box did. That's what John said to do in third John. There is no honor if it's not financial honor.

It makes me want to puke when a preacher of 50 years is retiring, recognized for a few minutes in a service, and then shown a video—a "tribute" that took only a few minutes to make. Then an announcement is made that there will be ice cream cake in the lobby for everyone. That minister preached the gospel for 50 years; we have a Dairy Queen ice cream cake for him. You either honor somebody or don't honor them.

There's no prosperity and there's no financial anointing without honor. The Shunammite woman didn't give to Elisha incorporated; she gave to Elijah. Maybe I have a different perspective because I'm a preacher's kid. But to me, the minister matters at least as much as the people he's ministering to. Because if he's gone, no one's getting ministered to. So, he should be cared for.

Another minister that I like, I sent money to him personally (not for his ministry). He sent me a message back saying, "thank you, this will be used prayerfully for the work of the Lord." I wrote, "I specifically told you it's not to be used for the work of the Lord, it's to be used for you, and you can do it un-prayerfully. You can spend it on ice cream for all I care. Go take your wife out and have a good time." A happy minister is a better preacher. You're going to get the best out of a vessel by taking care of the vessel.

Those that receive a prophet in the name of a prophet will receive a prophet's reward. What does that mean? Very few people receive a minister in the anointing. "Oh, that's Gary, the evangelist. That's Mike, the pastor. He's a good guy, he likes to hunt." They don't see them like they're carrying Jesus. You can't financially honor people like John G. Lake and Smith Wigglesworth because they're dead, but there are men in your generation who carry what those men carried and are sent to your generation. Who are they? How have you honored them? If you receive them as a prophet to your generation and honor them as a prophet, you will receive what God gives them.

Buy your pastor a car and watch what happens. Send your pastor on an all-expense-paid vacation to a five-star resort and watch what happens. When you honor a prophet, who's a real prophet, in the name of a prophet, it stirs their gift to head in your direction.

There's a pastor who's almost 90-years-old, and we send him a good chunk of money every month. Enough where if nothing else happened for him, he'd be able to live well. That's how it should be for somebody that preached for 60 years, and I love him. He called me the other day, and he said, "Jonathan, I just want you to know I've just been praying for you quite a bit and thanking the Lord for you." Do you think that factors into how smoothly things run for me? Because I made a point to honor one of God's great servants who is almost 90, now in his house, he's taken an hour or so every day to pray in tongues for me, to intercede for me. It's not magic. There are principles in this book that if you work them, they will work for you.

When I was growing up, my pastor acquired the church when it had 30-some people. He built it up to an 800-seat sanctuary that was full, for two different services every Sunday. It went from 30 to 1400 people, in a town of next to nobody.

The church had a parsonage, and he lived in it. He didn't own any land and didn't own his home because his home belonged to the church. So, if he was to retire and leave the church, he would have nothing and no way to buy a house. So, he wanted to buy the home from the church. They have a business meeting on a Sunday night where they said, "How much are we going to sell the home and the land to the pastor for?" My father's face got red, he lifted his hand, and they recognized him. My father, in a stern voice said, "The pastor took this church with about 30 people. We now have over 1,000 coming every Sunday. We have a Christian school. We have acreage. This church has millions of dollars in the bank, and we're going to vote on how much to sell him this home? Why don't we give him the home to honor him for all he has done by the grace of God?"

That comment sent the meeting in another direction. The elders took a vote with the congregation. They voted unanimously to gift that home and property to the pastor, a great man of God. They gave him the house.

About six years later, a lady called my father and said, "The Lord spoke to me to give you my home." Her home had seven acres, and it was beautiful. She turned it over to him, and the Lord spoke to my father, "Do you remember when you decided to honor your pastor by making sure that house was given to him? When you made that decision, I made a decision to give you your own home." What you make happen for others, God makes happen for you. The home and property given to my dad dwarfs that given to his pastor. It comes back multiplied.

You never go wrong by honoring God's servants. I've made it a point the last few years to send something substantial to anyone in the ministry who God has used to impact my life spiritually.

Whether he wears it or not, I don't know, but Bishop David Oyedepo has a Rolex I gave him worth almost $20,000. At the time, it was the most valuable thing I had. That watch was worth more than what I had in the bank put together. I gave it to him. His revelation on the Word of God changed my life. It's still changing my life. I feel indebted to people who sow into my life. Me giving that watch to Bishop Oyedepo wasn't me being nice. Where would I be without the grace of God that was on his life to minister the gospel to me?

The Bible doesn't teach mountains and valleys. It teaches glory to glory, victory to victory, and faith to faith. The Bible doesn't just teach us to honor God, it teaches us to also honor men of God. "Well, I don't have anything like that to give to people." Bull crap. You have something. God doesn't give people nothing, so start where you're at. It's a principle; it has nothing to do with how much money you have. It has to do with your heart. The old cliche is true; "If God can get it through you, God will get it to you." If God can ever find a vessel that doesn't plug up the flow, He will use it.

I've done everything in my power to honor Rodney Howard-Browne. He laid hands on me in 2011, and the next Sunday, our ministry exploded by every metric. You don't just say thank you. You do something. There is no love without giving. Solomon so loved that Solomon gave. David, I have set my affection on the temple, and so I have given. God so loved the world that He gave. There is no true love without giving. No chance. And your gift comes back to you.

Who has made a deep spiritual impact in your life? How have you honored them? Make a list. Once you get that account rectified, you're going to see things change in your life.

> I am not commanding you to do this. But I am testing how genuine your love is...
>
> — 2 CORINTHIANS 8:8

LAW FIFTEEN

THE LAW OF SIGNIFICANT SEED SOWING

Through the Law of Significant Seed Sowing, God can take you higher than your whole nation. There are already men like this that exist today, and they achieved their wealth without any help from God.

> "And now, because of my devotion to the Temple of my God, I am giving all of my own private treasures of gold and silver to help in the construction. This is in addition to the building materials I have already collected for his holy Temple. I am donating more than 112 tons of gold from Ophir and 262 tons of refined silver to be used for overlaying the walls of the buildings and for the other gold and silver work to be done by the craftsmen. Now then, who will follow my example and give offerings to the Lord today?"
> Then the family leaders, the leaders of the tribes of

> Israel, the generals and captains of the army, and the king's administrative officers all gave willingly. For the construction of the Temple of God, they gave about 188 tons of gold, 10,000 gold coins, 375 tons of silver, 675 tons of bronze, and 3,750 tons of iron. They also contributed numerous precious stones, which were deposited in the treasury of the house of the Lord under the care of Jehiel, a descendant of Gershon. The people rejoiced over the offerings, for they had given freely and wholeheartedly to the Lord, and King David was filled with joy.
>
> — 1 CHRONICLES 29:3-9

David gave 112 tons of gold. The entire rest of the nation gave 188 tons of gold. It took almost a whole nation to equal David. Now that's an offering! If you tally that up, you're probably over $10 billion in what the people gave, about $8 billion in what David gave. So, in one day, about $18 billion came in an offering to build God's house.

> After this prayer, the meeting place shook, and they were all filled with the Holy Spirit. Then they preached the word of God with boldness.
> All the believers were united in heart and mind. And they felt that what they owned was not their own, so they shared everything they had. The apostles testified powerfully to the resurrection of the Lord Jesus, and God's great blessing was upon them all. There were no needy people among them, because those who owned land or houses would

> sell them and bring the money to the apostles to give to those in need.
> For instance, there was Joseph, the one the apostles nicknamed Barnabas (which means "Son of Encouragement"). He was from the tribe of Levi and came from the island of Cyprus. He sold a field he owned and brought the money to the apostles.
>
> — ACTS 4:31-37

He sold a piece of land he owned and gave the whole amount to the apostles. In combining 1 Chronicles 29 and Acts 4, you see the law of significant seed sowing. We can also see an example of this law found in Genesis with Abraham and Isaac.

> Some time later, God tested Abraham's faith.
> "Abraham!" God called.
> "Yes," he replied. "Here I am."
> "Take your son, your only son—yes, Isaac, whom you love so much—and go to the land of Moriah. Go and sacrifice him as a burnt offering on one of the mountains, which I will show you."
>
> — GENESIS 22:1-2

There are times when God speaks to you about something you love and ask you to give it. Those are special times because it will change your financial level when God speaks to you about giving at a higher level. When God changes your level financially, you never go backward, unless you choose to duck out on your covenant. God will put you at a level that will make you think you had a lucky month.

Then it turns into a lucky two months. Then it turns into a lucky five months straight. And before too long, you realize, "I've changed levels. This isn't going backward. I didn't just have a great month and go back to normal, I changed levels."

When the COVID lockdowns hit the earth in 2020, I thought it would be a miracle if we lived through the year. Though I never let it come out of my mouth, I was certain there would at least be a retraction in 2020, since 2019 was a record year for us. But in 2020 we almost doubled 2019 in terms of giving, even with it being illegal to have church. Of course, we had church anyway, but nothing in our natural circumstances set us up for a great year, or a good year, or even basic survival.

You don't go backward when God sets your level unless you choose to go back. God has a way of changing your financial level. When God speaks to you about a precious seed, he has a permanent change of financial levels in mind.

We pick back up in Genesis 22:12…

> "Don't lay a hand on the boy!" the angel said. "Do not hurt him in any way, for now I know that you truly fear God. You have not withheld from me even your son, your only son."
> Then Abraham looked up and saw a ram caught by its horns in a thicket. So he took the ram and sacrificed it as a burnt offering in place of his son. Abraham named the place Yahweh-Yireh (which means "the Lord will provide"). To this day, people still use that name as a proverb: "On the mountain of the Lord it will be provided."
>
> — GENESIS 22:12-14

To this day, people still speak of this proverb: 'On the mountain of the Lord it will be provided.'

> Then the angel of the Lord called again to Abraham from heaven. "This is what the Lord says: Because you have obeyed me and have not withheld even your son, your only son, I swear by my own name that I will certainly bless you. I will multiply your descendants beyond number, like the stars in the sky and the sand on the seashore. Your descendants will conquer the cities of their enemies. And through your descendants all the nations of the earth will be blessed—all because you have obeyed me."
>
> — GENESIS 22:15-18

A generational blessing—*this seed that you sowed will cause your descendants to take cities.* That's not a 100-fold return, that's a higher level. Remember, that's what sowing is. That's why seed is precious to God, because it's obeying. When you sow seed, you're obeying God, and obedience is greater than sacrifice.

God didn't want Isaac. God wanted Abraham's heart. God wanted to ensure the things he had given Abraham had not taken God's place in Abraham's heart. That's what God does; as He blesses you, there are financial tests. He did this to test Abraham. God wants to see whether the things He's given you have taken His place in your life. When you prove they have not, it qualifies you for more and for blessings that money can't buy.

> When the Lord brought back his exiles to Jerusalem, it was like a dream! We were filled with laughter, and we sang for joy. And the other nations said, "What amazing things the Lord has done for them." Yes, the Lord has done amazing things for us! What joy!
> Restore our fortunes, Lord, as streams renew the desert. Those who plant in tears will harvest with shouts of joy. They weep as they go to plant their seed, but they sing as they return with the harvest.
>
> — PSALM 126:1-6

Tearful seed produces joyful harvest. They wept when they planted their seed. Have you ever planted seed that way? I have. When I was going to give all my money (and I mean all my money), knowing I wouldn't be paid for another 8 days, I didn't cry, but my blood pressure was up! It was difficult to sow that amount, and I was ready to not eat for eight days. Someone gave me $1,000 on the way back to my seat from sowing that seed.

I thought God was looking to starve me for eight days, but when God speaks to you about a seed, he already has your increase in mind. Offerings are not to increase the church and decrease the parishioner; offerings are something God instituted to increase his people.

I own the cattle on a thousand hills, says the Lord. *If I was hungry, would I ask you for food?* God doesn't require the help of any mortal man. God doesn't need our help.

When God speaks to us about giving, it's not because He's running a struggling nonprofit and needs help from you. No father ever needs help from their children. No good father ever solicits financial help from his children. Can you imagine me going to my eight-year-old daughter, "Camila, it's the beginning of a new month. Bills are due. You use this house as much as anyone does. We actually spend the majority of our gasoline driving you around. So, chip in." No, nobody in their right mind does that. No proper father does that, and neither does God.

> But there was a certain man named Ananias who, with his wife, Sapphira, sold some property. He brought part of the money to the apostles, claiming it was the full amount. With his wife's consent, he kept the rest.
>
> — ACTS 5:1-2

I was with a minister when he sowed his Rolex to another minister. I was with him in his office about nine years later when an usher came in and said, "A man gave this box to you." He opened it up, it was a Rolex with the box and papers. I watched him open a safe and put that Rolex in with seven other luxury watches. Most of them were Rolex's. He said to me, "Do you remember when I gave my Rolex away nine years ago? These have all been given to me since then." He never had one given to him before that. What you sow, you reap. What you never sow, you never reap.

If you find yourself saying, "That must be nice, I'd like to have that given to me," what have you given? If you don't like your harvest, change your seed.

When you have something you love, and the Lord asks you to give it, He's seeing whether you mirror His nature or not. God didn't send some angel to die for our sins, God gave His only Son as a sacrifice. In return, He has received back hundreds of millions of sons. He wants to see if you'll follow His example. That's what He was checking with Abraham. "See if you will give the son you love, like I will." And the Bible says it's a mirror of God giving Christ. He already crossed the bridge in his heart, "I'm done." But he believed God would raise Isaac back from the dead because God said it would be through Isaac that His promises would be fulfilled. The whole thing was done in faith. When I speak to you about giving, I try to keep you in faith, not conscious of need, but conscious of faith.

I had a guy come to me one time and say, "I have a piece of land the Lord spoke to me to give to a ministry. I want to give it to you if you'll put a tent on it and have a crusade."

Either give it, or don't. You're not going to give it to me and then tell me how to use it. So, I said, "Keep it."

When you're ready to give, give. You don't give with strings attached. "Hey Dad, I'm going to give you my Rolex. But in your will, give it back to me after you die."

Give it. If you give it, you totally release it.

Some people will make their own nonprofit as a creative way to avoid giving when God prospers them. Suppose a man's wife receives an inheritance of $3 million, and the man thinks, "I'm not giving $300,000 to my church. What are they going to do with it? I don't even really like my church's direction lately. My wife has always wanted to help stop human trafficking. So, my wife is going to start a human trafficking ministry."

The foundation of your new ministry is "not wanting to give." So, you made your own ministry where you could give your money to that ministry. You didn't want to give it to your church, so you started your own nonprofit. People find creative ways where they've technically tithed, can still get the tax break, but all they did was transfer money from their personal account to another account they control.

You have four groups of Christians; those that don't give, those who find creative ways to avoid truly giving, and those who give but never enter into the law of significant seed. Then there's a fourth category I believe you fall into: those who obey the Lord when it comes to significant seed. I've done that several times. I'm glad I did. It changed our level again and again.

Sowing significant seed sets you apart. To the true giver, there's no reservoir. Everything just passes through. The old saying is, "Your sowing will always outperform your savings." Some people try to accumulate material wealth. The easiest way is to sow and obey God when he speaks to you concerning significant seed.

One of the first examples of this happened when I gave a challenge one night for people to sow something significant to them. I may have never done this before or since, but I told people, "I'm not going to receive an offering tonight. I want you to take 24 hours, and when we come back tomorrow night, I want you to bring whatever personally represents a significant seed." Well, one young man, who I think was in third grade at that time, brought a clear plastic sandwich bag full of his dollars and coins from his piggy bank. He and his parents told me that was the money he was saving to go to his first NFL football game. I think it was around $280, if I remember right. At first, he planned to give some, and then he told his parents he decided to give it all. His heart's greatest desire was to go to an NFL football game, and he almost had all the money saved. $280 is a lot of money to save when you're eight years old. It took me until I was in my mid 20s to save up that much, and he gave it all.

If you had traditional church teaching, you would think, "Well, he made a choice to support the work of the Lord instead of going to the football game. God will make it up to him in Heaven when he sees how many lives he's touched." But that's not how God works, as many of us know. The next weekend his father got a call from a man with a corporate box at that football team's stadium. The box had an all-you-can-eat buffet, indoor seating with a TV, and an outdoor seating option to watch the game. The man with the corporate box said, "I allow my son to take one friend with him when we go to the games, and my son chose to take your son. If it's all right, I'd like to take him, not to one game, but to all eight home games this year." The boy gave up his money for one cheap seat and instead received eight trips to the luxury box. That is a perfect illustration of how God works. When he asks you to give what's precious to you, he floods you with greater blessing because you've passed the heart test.

My daughter, Camila, had two people give her a $100 bill in one night, which in itself is a miracle when you're seven. My wife said to her, "How much of that belongs to God?" Because she didn't know how to figure out what 10% was, she said, "I'll give Him one and I'll keep one." But when it came time to give, she did what the other boy did and said, "I'll give both." She puts $200 in.

I go to my next meeting, and the pastor's wife comes to me at the end of the meeting and says, "Our children's church took an offering for your daughter every night you were here." They were having a children's revival during my revival. The offering was received at the children's revival every night for my daughter. I'd never had that happen to me as a preacher's kid, and I never had it happen to Camila in seven years of traveling. What a coincidence that it happened after she gave all she had.

The offering was $440, and they rounded it up to $500. On my way home, I stopped at a different meeting that I wasn't preaching at. A businessman came to me and said, "The Lord spoke to me to give

$5,000 to you and your wife. I know this might sound strange, but the Lord also spoke to me to give $1,000 to your daughter." I still wasn't over people giving $200 to a seven-year-old. Who gives $1,000? I came home after that trip, eight days after Camila gave her $200, and I said, "Hey, Camila, do you remember that $200 you gave?" I showed her the checks, saying, "You now have 15 of those $100 bills. They're yours." And she said, "Cool," and kept playing.

That did something to me, but it didn't seem like it mattered for her. Maybe it did more for me than her. My daughter doesn't have any needs, she doesn't have college tuition, she's not in debt, she doesn't have a car payment, she doesn't have a phone payment, she doesn't have a mortgage.

The law of seed, time, and harvest has no respect for what age you are, what color you are, how much you need help or don't need help. The law of sowing and reaping just works for whoever will work it. When a farmer puts seed into the ground, the ground doesn't care what needs he has. The ground doesn't care if he's Black, or Hispanic, or Indian, or White, or First Nations, Native American, Samoan, or Japanese. The ground doesn't care. The ground receives the seed and then brings forth the harvest in due season; 30, 60, or 100-fold.

At one of my meetings, there was a boy who had chickens he bought with his own money. After the night service, he came to me and handed me an envelope with $1,000 in it. It was all his money he earned from taking care of chickens, collecting their eggs, and selling their eggs at the farmer's market. He gave it all to me. Do you know what his mother wrote to me a couple of weeks later? What do you think she said?

"I want my son's money back. How dare you take advantage of a little boy?"

No, this is what she said, "Hi there. I just wanted to let you know that since our eight-year-old son sowed his seed, all his makings from his egg sales, the chickens have gone from producing 12 to 16 eggs a day to 28 to 30 eggs a day. God is always true to His Word. Thank you for accepting his seed and taking him seriously. We are thankful for our son. We know God has mighty plans for him. We love you guys. Our lives have truly changed since the meetings in DeLand, Florida."

That's how it works. It doesn't matter whether you're my kid, that kid, or whether you're an adult. Originally, this kid was going to give $300, his mother told me that when he saw the videos of the people getting saved in our meetings, he said, "If that's what the money goes to, then I want to give all my money." That was a significant seed sown due to love for God and His Kingdom.

Your place at the top is guaranteed when your heart is moved by what moves God's heart, and you prove it with your giving.

I knew five years ago that our ministry was heading for a place that would require a personal aircraft. We would require a jet, and I knew I didn't have anywhere near enough money to even use personal aircraft. So, I considered, "What do I need to do? What seed do I have that could provoke that type of harvest?" I didn't have near enough money to sow to bring forth a jet as a 100-fold return. As I was driving and thinking about that, I realized I was in a relatively new Cadillac Escalade that our ministry owned. It was paid off, I bought it with cash. I thought, "I have a vehicle. I require a plane. I'll sow the vehicle and believe for a private aircraft."

I didn't sow it right away. It took me 24 hours, because I got it washed, waxed, and detailed. I took the title and the keys, drove it to the pastor I was preaching for that night, and I said, "Have you ever seen my Cadillac Escalade?"

He said, "Yeah."

I said, "Do you like it?"

He said, "Yeah."

I said, "It's yours."

His eyes got big, and he said, "Seriously?"

I said, "Yeah."

I had to get a ride home that night with my brother-in-law. That's the first time I had somebody give me a ride since I was like 15. Somebody asked me after I gave it, "What are you going to do for transportation now?"

"I don't know. I'll figure it out tomorrow. For transportation tonight, I'm going to have my brother-in-law give me a ride home."

This last year and a half, I've taken personal aircraft everywhere I've traveled. I didn't have to wear a mask, didn't have to have my body searched, unaffected by the pilot shortage in America, and could spend two extra days home a week. That wasn't an accident. That was provoked by a roughly $60,000 seed.

Significant harvests are provoked by significant seed. Where are you believing to go in life? What level seems to have alluded your grasp? What seed do you have in your hand right now that could provoke the type of harvest you're believing for?

You hear many Christians say, "I'm believing for a house." Well, there's a type of seed that provokes a house, and there's a type of seed that doesn't provoke a house.

If you're believing for a plane, like I was, $100 isn't going to get you there. I loved that vehicle. I loved riding in it, and it was very comfortable. But as comfortable as that vehicle was, it can't take me from Pittsburgh to New Mexico in three hours. With a plane, a 20-hour drive turns into one hour with time zone changes. I can wake up in my own bed Sunday morning and be in the pulpit in New Mexico one hour later. You can't beat that. You can take what you have right now and keep it, and it's your harvest. But if you sow it, it goes and creates a future for you, the type of future your money can't buy.

Years ago, I believed God for a huge financial increase because I wanted to do outdoor soul-winning crusades. I knew I'd have to pay for them myself because churches don't usually have money, and if they do, they're certainly not going to use it to help you in your soul-winning crusade. Many times, churches are upset that you're even in the city. I met with pastors in the city one time about doing a soul-winning crusade, you would have thought I was trying to get them to help me open a strip club, and I wasn't even asking for money. I needed pastors to follow up on the people after I left. Not interested. So, I knew I would have to make it happen myself, and I didn't have the money to do outdoor crusades. They cost $125,000 to $140,000 apiece. I did not have that in the budget.

This was on my mind as I was driving to go teach. We were in prayer and fasting to start the year in January. I popped on social media to listen to some preaching, and I listened to a replay of a broadcast another evangelist did. There's no way he could have seen me log on because he wasn't live, he already did the broadcast. I fast-forwarded to about the 22-minute mark, because I wanted to skip the online greetings and just hear the Word. I kid you not, as I'm driving, the man says this, "There's a young evangelist listening to me right now."

I thought, "Okay." He didn't say a young preacher; he said a young evangelist. There's not a lot of those.

"You're believing God for great financial increase for your ministry right now."

I'm listening. "I'm getting ready to go on one last tour around the United States, and I want to go on a tour bus."

"If you'll sow $1,000 to help this old man take one more tour around the country, the Lord will give you $100,000 before the end of this month."

Like many of you, I grew up thinking it's a scam if a preacher starts talking like that. But I also know a thing or two about odds. So, I looked at it from a gambling perspective. This man is giving me 100 to one odds. If he's lying, I lose $1,000. If he's telling the truth and he heard from the Lord, I get $100,000. I'm willing to roll the dice on that one. I'm half-joking. But it registered with my spirit so, I did it.

My last meeting for that month was January 29th, and it was a Friday night. The church was packed, and I thought, "This is going to be the night the money comes in the offering; what that guy said will come true." Well, I get the offering, not only did $100,000 NOT come in that night, but the offering for the whole week was low. I thought, "Shoot. Well, enjoy your $1,000. You're a good guy anyway. I enjoy listening to you." The next morning, we checked the mail, and on the last day of the month, there was an anonymous check for $100,000. I never told anybody what happened in the vehicle. ...totally insane, just like the Lord said.

At some point, you have to make up your mind; do you want to listen to other people's stories, or do you want to join hands with God and write your own story?

Everyone's seed is different. For one boy, it was his football ticket money. For the little boy, it was his egg money. For me in Nigeria, it was my Rolex watch. Another time it was my car. But you're making a mistake if you let your life go by and never decide, "You know what? I'm going to turn my faith loose through a seed."

I'll tell you this too; I sowed that Cadillac Escalade in 2016. The planes started to become a reality in 2020. Let your seed germinate in the ground. If you don't have a harvest within 12 hours, relax. Sometimes it will come in 24 hours, within the same hour, by the end of the month. But some things, like Abraham with Isaac, you actually lay up an inheritance for your children.

LAW SIXTEEN

THE LAW OF DILIGENCE

The Bible says the anointing brings wealth that's hidden from other people to you. This wealth comes through The Law of Diligence.

> This is what the Lord says to Cyrus, his anointed one, whose right hand he will empower. Before him, mighty kings will be paralyzed with fear. Their fortress gates will be opened, never to shut again.
>
> — ISAIAH 45:1

The anointing opens mighty gates that no one else can open. They will be open, never to shut again.

> "I will go before you, Cyrus, and level the mountains. I will smash down gates of bronze and cut through bars of iron. And I will give you treasures hidden

> in the darkness—secret riches. I will do this so you may know that I am the Lord, the God of Israel, the one who calls you by name."
>
> — ISAIAH 45:2-3

There is a financial anointing, and the Bible says: *It opens fortress gates. And I will give you treasures hidden in darkness. Secret riches.* Who did the Lord say this to? Cyrus, His anointed one whose right hand He will empower.

The anointing brings wealth. God knows where all the money is. God knows where all the gold is. God knows where all the oil is. God knows what land will decrease in value and what land is going to increase.

> Do you see any truly competent workers? They will serve kings rather than working for ordinary people.
>
> — PROVERBS 22:29

I'm going to break the law of diligence into five parts.

But first, sometimes, the best way to understand something is to understand what it isn't. The antonyms for diligent are: careless; thoughtless; uncareful; unenthusiastic; indifferent; lethargic; and negligent. You could probably check all these boxes for most businesses in America.

Most businesses are poorly run in the wake of the COVID lockdowns; they're careless, thoughtless, uncareful, unenthusiastic, indifferent, languid, lethargic, and often negligent. That's the majority of

American workers, especially in the service industry. This is NOT diligence.

Meanwhile, some politicians want the minimum wage increased. Go to a drive-through at a restaurant and tell me why wages should be increased. Based on demonstrated diligence, there's no basis for increased wages.

If I were to start a business, I'm sure I could put all of my competitors out of business very quickly. Because I'm a Christian, I believe in diligence. When people visit Revival Today, they often remark how happy, joyful, and enthusiastic everybody is. It's a Christian trait.

Whatever work you put your hands to, do it with all your might. That's what Joseph did in slavery, for crying out loud. That's what Joseph did in prison. And what happened every time? He rose to the top, and by the law of diligence, it took him out of prison—and standing before kings.

If I call Joel Osteen's church right now—the largest church in America—do you think the phone will ring 11 times and then go, "The voicemail of the person you're trying to reach is full. Thank you. Goodbye." No. I guarantee I'll get a happy person on the phone. I've never tried it, but I can guarantee this because I know how people operate. When people are diligent, every aspect of what they do is diligent. On the other hand, if I call a church that has a handful of people and has been that way for 20 years, no one will pick up, and the follow-up will go something like this:

"Hey, I tried to call, and nobody answered."

"We're closed on Mondays."

"Why are you closed on Mondays? Took a lot out of you delivering that 23-minute speech on Sunday? Needed a full 48 hours to recuperate before you could get back in? You closed your whole office down? You can't hire one person to answer the phone? You can't have somebody forward the church phone to their personal phone through an app? I don't understand."

Tell me why a coffee shop closes at 2:00 PM. Do you hate money? Now, I understand if you want to be a specialty place; breakfast only, or something like that. If I had a coffee place, I'd be open 24 hours. There's money you're missing.

There are restaurants still listed online as open until 9:00 PM, yet when you go there, they closed two hours prior, and there's a sign that reads, "Closed because of COVID." What does COVID have to do with you closing two hours early? Did all your employees' lungs seize up and die at 7:00 PM? Or did you use something like COVID as an excuse to be lazy?

Most people don't work hard. Solomon addresses it in the Bible. The Bible addresses hard work. Solomon, the wealthiest man who ever lived, said there's a part of acquiring wealth that requires hard work. It doesn't feel like hard work if you're doing the right thing. Most days, I broadcast three times before the day is over, and all of the broadcasts require preparation.

I enjoy doing my job as a minister. The Bible says *the sower sows the Word*. You're not going to find too many days that I'm not sowing the Word. If I'm not doing it personally, the "digital me" is doing it on social media and television every day. I set that up. If I was in business, I'd do the same thing. Whatever I set out to do, I do it very well.

I have a friend in construction who's too busy; he has more clients than he can take because he works hard. He finishes a job before the deadline he gives people. That's diligence.

THE 20 LAWS THAT GOVERN THE FINANCIAL ANOINTING

#1: DILIGENCE IS HARD WORK

Whatever your hand finds to do, do it with all your might. Hard work. Paul said in the New Testament, in the New Living Translation: *We work hard and suffer much.*

You can't be a bum. Your life can't revolve around taking care of your pet if you're going to rise to the top. Can you imagine somebody inviting me to preach… "I'd love to come to your church, but we have a dog now, and he's just a puppy, and we're still getting him trained." That's how people are; not only do they tie their lives to things unrelated to their purpose, they tie their lives to things that detract from their purpose.

In the United States, it's easy to fall into the trap of lethargy because you actually don't have to work very hard in this country to have everything you want. People living in Section 8 housing have flat-screen 4K televisions. They have Wi-Fi. They have climate control. They have food. Unless you have an abusive parent and you're a child, very few people in America wonder whether they can eat today. You don't have to do much to keep your head above water in America. If you're not careful, you'll become a bum.

The goal is not to simply survive. The goal is to be great. God put greatness on you when He anointed you, and for that greatness to come to bear, it will require hard work. Again, it shouldn't feel like torture doing what God's called you to do. It should be enjoyable. If it's not enjoyable to a degree, then you're not doing the right thing.

Many people have heard messages from ministers contradicting what I'm saying. This is because Revelation 3 says laziness and lukewarmness will creep into preaching. They'll say "I mean, it's not about what we do. It's about what He's done. Many people think you have to strive to get ahead, but it's His grace that makes it happen." But this is what the Apostle Paul had to say…

> Because of God's grace to me, I have laid the foundation like an expert builder. Now others are building on it. But whoever is building on this foundation must be very careful. For no one can lay any foundation other than the one we already have—Jesus Christ.
>
> — 1 CORINTHIANS 3:10-11

> After all, who is Apollos? Who is Paul? We are only God's servants through whom you believed the Good News. Each of us did the work the Lord gave us. I planted the seed in your hearts, and Apollos watered it, but it was God who made it grow. It's not important who does the planting, or who does the watering. What's important is that God makes the seed grow. The one who plants and the one who waters work together with the same purpose. And both will be rewarded for their own hard work.
>
> — 1 CORINTHIANS 3:5-8

You'll be rewarded by God for what? Not His grace, but hard work. Some people think a person's works don't matter. What do you think we will lay before the Lord during the Bema judgment? The Bible says each man will present his works to the Lord and will be judged accordingly. Some works will be like wood, hay, and stumble and won't pass through the fire. Others will be like gold, silver, and precious stones, and the builder will be well-rewarded for their hard work.

This is an interesting scripture for the people that say, "It's not about us striving, bro. It's about His grace…"

> But whatever I am now, it is all because God poured out his special favor on me—and not without results. For I have worked harder than any of the other apostles; yet it was not I but God who was working through me by his grace.
>
> — 1 CORINTHIANS 15:10

God's grace empowers you to do great works. The American preachers get an A for effort. "It's not about works, bro. It's about grace." But you can't separate grace and works. God poured out His grace upon me and not without results. What was the result? When God poured His grace out on Paul, it caused him to labor more intensely than all the other apostles. It's probably why I work hard without feeling like I'm doing any work; it's God's grace.

Rodney Howard-Browne holds 10 hours of services a day, and he's fresh as a daisy. That's grace. It's grace to finish a meeting late at night, get on a plane, fly through the night, preach straight off the plane in the morning, and have fun doing it. God's grace empowers you to work hard and outwork others.

"Man, I don't know how you do that." When you hear somebody say that to you, you know you're starting to tap into God's grace. When you hear somebody complaining about everything they're doing, you know they don't have any grace. "I have to fly four hours tomorrow, and when I get off the plane, I'm in meetings immediately and…"

Yeah, I don't hear any grace working. Life should be an exciting adventure you eagerly look forward to each day. If you're not, something's wrong. You're likely out of God's purpose and out of His will.

Hard work is a part of the law of diligence, and I want to be clear, hard work is not being busy.

"I do work hard. I have to take my kids to school in the morning, and then I have to go pick up a cake because I volunteered to be the homeroom mother, and we're having a party at school. And then I have to take her there, and I have to be at the party. And then I have to take my daughter directly to gymnastics. She has a recital."

Everything you've mentioned is just errands. They have nothing to do with actions that produce something. So don't confuse overloading your life with parties and sports, as being hard work. Hard work is not busy work. Hard work is working hard in the assignment God's given you, things pertaining to your calling; it's not busyness, it's hard work.

#2: DILIGENCE IS HONEST WORK

Under the law of diligence, it's not just hard work, because there's lots of people who work hard but have no money. In economics, we call them the working poor. There are certain businesses where even though you work 60 hours a week, you're still never going to get ahead.

The minimum wage in Pennsylvania is $7.25 an hour at this writing. So, let's say you work hard; you not only work a 40-hour week at $7.25 an hour, you pick up 20 hours extra. Once the government takes their cut, federal and state, your take-home pay a week will be around $390. You'll make around $20,000 a year, which is well below the poverty line. If you had a spouse and they did the same thing, you'd have just over $40,000 a year. With two people and kids, that's not going to cut it. Hard work alone is not sufficient.

With a few exceptions, your job, by itself, is not going to be your pathway to riches. If you play quarterback in the NFL or if you're the CEO of a pharmaceutical company, you are an exception. Most likely, your paycheck will be seed money to sow and start a business or a side-hustle that the Lord gives you to generate your wealth.

Number two, honest work. To work smarter, not harder is the opposite of what I'm teaching. I'm telling you it's not work smart *instead* of hard, it's doing *both*. Those are little cliches. If you listen to what I teach, it'll help you. It's work smarter *and* harder. Working wisely is not a substitute for working hard, producing much, and maximizing each day.

Part of being a diligent businessperson is being honest in your work. I mentioned a friend of mine who works in construction. Part of the reason he's running circles around this competition is because he keeps his word on what he charges his customers. The price remains the number he quoted, or it's lower. It's standard practice in America for a contractor to tell you the job will cost $40,000, then halfway through, they say, "Something came up," and now it's going to be $51,000. They always raise the price halfway through, and then you're screwed because if you say, "No, I'm not paying that." Then they say, "Okay, then we can't complete the job," and you're left with a half-finished home. That's par for the course in the construction industry. He doesn't do that.

Whatever industry you're in, there are dishonest practices. Part of being a Christian who operates in the financial anointing is making up your mind to not participate in slimy behavior. "I don't care if that's how things are done here in this business, I'm going to do what's right, not what you're allowed to do." Honest work. I'll be there when I say I'm going to be there. I'll charge what I said I'm going to charge. I'll complete the work I said I would complete. No excuses. When people realize they can trust you and you have credibility, word spreads fast. You couldn't hire an advertising firm that will advertise for you as much as word of mouth about the honest worker that lives in their city.

#3: DILIGENCE IS SMART WORK

Smart work. God gave Truett Cathy, the founder of Chick-fil-A, one of the most ingenious ideas I've ever heard. God gave him a Scripture upon which he built Chick-fil-A: *A good name is valued above riches.* And the Lord gave him the revelation that a business needs to have a good name. In other words, your business needs to be thought well of. God will give you revelation pertaining to what He has you do. The last I looked, Burger King averages $1.1 million per franchise. Chick-fil-A averages $4 million per franchise. It quadruples Burger King in revenue per franchise despite being closed one day a week while Burger King's open all seven.

When you go to other fast-food restaurants, you're often exposed to unpleasant experiences. Sometimes the people aren't even wearing a uniform.

"Can I help you? ...we're out of that."

You get treated basically the same as if you broke into someone's kitchen and demanded they make you a meal. Nobody wants to be there. Everything's sloppy. When you go to Chick-fil-A, you're greeted by some of the kindest and most respectful people you'll ever meet. Well, why does that happen? Why does one place have really good employees, and another has bottom-of-the-barrel workers?

Do you know the idea God gave Truett Cathy? God gave Truett Cathy the idea that whoever owns a Chick-fil-A franchise has to personally work at that franchise for a minimum number of hours per week. So, if I'm the 55-year-old wealthy owner and I have to be at the store, what type of people do you think I'll hire? There will be a quality of people I expect to hire and a certain quality person I won't allow. It would irritate me to see some slob coming in 10 minutes late and speaking disrespectfully to a customer while I've got 2 million dollars invested in the store.

Just one idea that God gave Truett Cathy made his restaurant blaze past his competition, and that's just one of them. The owner being on the premises is wisdom. If you own a business, you better be there. When the cat's away, the mice will play. To employees, it's just a job to make money. But to you, your life and reputation are on the line, and people should treat it accordingly.

I specifically remember a restaurant in an airport with a huge line, and the hostess announced, "Excuse me, everybody. We have a huge line. There are other restaurants. Please go there." I'm telling you, if I was the owner, she'd have been fired before she finished the sentence. "Please don't support our business. Please take your money elsewhere." Hey stupid, do you think you should make an announcement to tell people to go to other restaurants, or should you get on the phone and call in more workers? Do you know what a diligent worker would say? "I know the line seems long, but we're going to serve you fast. I guarantee that you're going to have better food than any of those other places." One idea God gave Truett Cathy caused him to repel the entire downfall of the American food industry—jerk employees that don't care about people, the food, or making the correct order.

When Abraham began ranching cattle, God gave him an idea. "Hey Abraham, you know how everybody in the whole world goes around looking for water? Would you like to know where there's a ton of water they don't know about? Under the ground. Start digging." Abraham is the first person on record in history to dig wells. Digging wells gave him several advantages over his competitors, the Canaanites.

Number one, they had to go look for water. Abraham could be at the same place with his cattle, 9:00 am to 5:00 pm every day.

Number two, his land was irrigated. So, in the time of drought, his land was fertile. If it quit raining, he wasn't dependent upon rain. The idea God gives you will remove the control of external circumstances and cause a wellspring for your livelihood.

Number three, when people had to take their cows in search of water, it made their cattle thinner because they were walking all day. Abraham's cattle could graze and become fat.

God will give you your own idea if you wait upon Him. He'll give you His wisdom. Combining God-given ideas and wisdom with honest, smart, hard work and tying these threads together makes you a diligent worker. The Bible says *you won't serve mere men; you'll serve kings.*

> "Bring all the tithes into the storehouse so there will be enough food in my Temple. If you do," says the Lord of Heaven's Armies, "I will open the windows of heaven for you. I will pour out a blessing so great you won't have enough room to take it in! Try it! Put me to the test!"
>
> — MALACHI 3:10

Windows are for looking through. He didn't say, "See if I won't open the floodgates of heaven and pour out a blessing." He didn't say, "See if I won't unlock the bank vault door." He said: *See if I won't open the windows of heaven.* When you tithe and give offerings, it allows you to look through God's windows. God will cause you to see what He knows, and that's why wisdom produces wealth.

One idea, one revelation from God, will put you ahead of all your competitors. God knew there was water underground. Nobody else knew it. Abraham, a tither, saw through that window and knew there was water under the ground.

We were one of the first ministries to broadcast live on social media. Flipping through Facebook years ago, I saw somebody was speaking, and it said "Live" blinking in red. When I saw it, I called Rom, and I said, "Find out how we can do that." The day came when Facebook Live was open to everyone, and we already had the equipment ready to go. We bought it all ahead of time. I knew that would be huge.

Are you kidding me? Instead of paying a quarter million a year to go on television, I can just turn my phone on or turn a camera on, link it up, and reach thousands of people for free? I knew it would be big if I put my services on livestream, and we were one of the first to do that. People would watch, then they would come, which helped grow the meetings. One idea. God will put things in front of your eyes that no one else has seen and give you a leg up.

#4: DILIGENCE IS CONSISTENT WORK

If you could go back in time and watch me at 24-years-old, I'm doing the exact same thing right now. It's just on a bigger scale, I'm better at it, and I've implemented more things to help get the message out. I've not changed my doctrine. I've not changed my focus. If you learn to stay with the thing God gave you and not allow new, exciting, and attractive things to pull you off course, you'll do great.

People too often quit their assignments. They're not consistent. How many people do you hear at the beginning of the year in the ministry, "We're going to start doing a podcast every day." They do it for about four days, then there's no podcast for six months. How many blogs are on a ministry website that started in 2016. There was a new blog post for about five or six posts, then there was a four-month break, and there hasn't been another one since.

Things are exciting when you begin. The excitement quickly fades. You have to develop a routine in a system, whether you feel motivated or not. That's why I like systems because a system takes motivation out of the equation. If I went to the gym only when I felt motivated, I would never go to the gym. But if I book six appointments a week and pay the money, I have to be at the gym. Otherwise, it means I will stand up my trainer if I don't show up. It no longer matters whether I feel like going to the gym. I have to be there. If we set an 11 o'clock broadcast time, it doesn't matter whether I feel like doing broadcasts or not; I'm on at 11 o'clock. You set up systems that pertain to your end goal, and you stay with it. You do it when you're excited to do it; you do it when you're not excited to do it. You just do it. You mark out a straight path for your feet and then stay on the path.

> Look straight ahead, and fix your eyes on what lies before you. Mark out a straight path for your feet; stay on the safe path. Don't get sidetracked; keep your feet from following evil.
>
> — PROVERBS 4:25-27

Don't get sidetracked. I don't understand why I meet someone who says they are a preacher, and now they're a multi-level marketer. They don't preach; they just sell stuff—I don't get why people do that.

You set a destination for your life that the Lord gives you. Then, it's not just about knowing the destination, the Bible also says to mark out a straight path for your feet. What path leads to that destination? Stay on the path.

There's a lot of good things that don't pertain to my path. I avoid them. It's not wrong, but it's wrong for me. There's a lot of things that seem good, but they're not your assignment.

When Americans were stranded in Afghanistan, I never sent any money to help evacuate them. Do you know why? I'm glad people did. I think it's great that people did. That's not my path. My ministry is not about evacuating American citizens out of other countries. That has nothing to do with me. What happens is that people in ministry get sidetracked.

There are always fads that come up in ministry. It was human trafficking ministry for a few years, then giving water bottles and socks to the homeless. There's all this new stuff that comes up. And there's people called to do those things, but not necessarily you. If the Devil can't sidetrack you with bad things, he'll try to sidetrack you with good things. Remember that.

When Bishop Oyedepo visited Yonggi Cho in South Korea, he became extremely bothered by how little Christianity there was in Japan. There was an extremely small percentage of preachers in that great country, so he started a church. The church wasn't growing. One day when he was praying, the Lord said to him, "Though there's a great need here, you are not the one I'm sending. Get back to Africa."

Need does not constitute a calling. Sex traffic victims need rescuing. Hungry children need feeding. There are endless needs on planet Earth, but you're only called to do one thing. If the Devil can't sidetrack you with bad things, such as drugs, alcohol, or perversion, he will sidetrack you with good things, something good that God didn't call you to do.

> But as the believers rapidly multiplied, there were rumblings of discontent. The Greek-speaking believers complained about the Hebrew-speaking believers, saying that their widows were being discriminated against in the daily distribution of food.
> So the Twelve called a meeting of all the believers. They said, "We apostles should spend our time teaching the word of God, not running a food program. And so, brothers, select seven men who are well respected and are full of the Spirit and wisdom. We will give them this responsibility. Then we apostles can spend our time in prayer and teaching the word."
>
> — ACTS 6:1-4

One of the first ways Satan tried to stop the multiplication of the early church was to get Peter to run a food program, pulling him away from prayer and ministry of the Word. Is it wrong to feed hungry widows? No, it's a command in scripture. Peter didn't say we're not feeding widows; Peter said to put other people in charge. I'm to be given to prayer and the ministry of the Word. Peter knew what caused them to lay the sick in the streets so a shadow might fall across them. If they were pulled out of prayer and ministry of the Word, the engine of the early church would fail.

Don't get sidetracked. People in the ministry get sidetracked. They get bored with the ministry, and they start doing other stuff. People in business get sidetracked and go into ministry when they shouldn't. They just get bored with their business and want to become an assistant pastor. Or they'll go to a church where their goal is to plant 20 churches in the next 10 years. Basically, they're just grabbing any man in the church that's solid. They have no call to the ministry; they're just a good guy. Think if they were running a $2 million business. In the next 10 to 20 years, the Lord might have taken it to $25 or $50 million, but they got sidetracked. The Lord never changed His plan. Stay on the path. Don't get sidetracked.

Ministry's a good thing. Other than me, you're not going to hear too many ministers discourage you from going into the ministry. We need missionaries. We need more evangelists. We need more Holy Ghost-filled pastors. But if you're not one that God's called to be a pastor, and He's given you an anointing for business, you are stepping out of your business to fill a need for which you don't possess an anointing. People will pat you on the back. People will think it's great you left your business. "Wow, he left. He was making millions, and now he's pastoring." And God's up in heaven going, "Yeah, I never told him to." God doesn't look to get the least out of you. God looks to maximize you. Don't get bored if you're in the ministry. If you're in business, don't get bored with your business.

People reinvent themselves 19 times. It takes a lifetime to get to a high level. If you change what you're doing every six years, you're never going anywhere. Some people were into healing in their ministry, then into soaking in God's presence, and then into worship nights. So even if you don't leave the ministry, you have to figure out what you do and stay with that. Any great minister, at the mention of their name, will make you think of what they are known for: Billy Graham, souls; Oral Roberts, healing; Kenneth Hagin, faith. They each had one thing.

Now think of this with me since we've used enough negative examples. If I listen to a message from Kenneth Hagin from the year 2000, what topic do you think he's going to cover? Faith. If I find a message from Kenneth Hagin in the 1960s, what message will he be speaking on? Faith. He never changed. Billy Graham never changed. Billy Graham could have done a million things, but he stayed preaching the simple message of salvation. He was a very wise man, very intelligent. Do you think he preached salvation because he only had a surface knowledge of the Bible and didn't know about deeper things? No, he knew all the deeper stuff. You can't allow yourself to get distracted in your calling.

#5: DILIGENCE HAS AN APPEARANCE

Man judges the outward appearance. God judges the heart. God is not your clientele; man is. Mankind will make up their mind about you, what you're doing, and your business, based on appearance. How your ministry appears matters just as how your business appears matters, and your personal appearance matters.

On Sunday mornings, our church platform doesn't look like it's laundry day. A slob-spirit has come into the church in America where everybody looks like a bum. I'm going in the other direction because appearance matters. When churches were strong in America, the platform looked excellent. When the church got weak in America, the platform looked like a pack of slobs.

Things that pertain to you should look excellent. Buildings should look excellent. I want my two buildings to look like the two best office buildings in town. I'm a Christian. I represent God. Things shouldn't be falling apart. It should be fresh blacktop, new siding, sharp paint, and clean windows. It's not like we have customers coming in here. It's a principle; things should look sharp. Everything should look excellent.

Carry yourself like you are already where you want to go, not like where you are now. As an evangelist, when I had a meeting at a dumpy looking church with barely any people, the natural instinct was to dress down to that level. Go the other direction. Make people ask, "Why is this person here? Why did he agree to come to this place?" Don't drop to the level of the place you're in. Stand out. Let me tell you something. If you get pulled over by a policeman, and you're wearing a tuxedo, you'll get treated differently than if you're wearing a hat on backwards. You say, "Well, that shouldn't be how things are." Well, that is how things are. God said so. Man judges by outward appearance. Why not make it work for you?

Think about my show, "Check the News." The studio was not cheap. Now think of this: If I did "Check the News" from my dining room table with a poor-quality camera, no microphone, and horrible sound, people would turn it on and say, "Oh, this guy's nuts. Oh, this guy's a COVID denier. Some lunatic in his kitchen." It could still be the same me, saying the same stuff, but because of the excellent background, the microphone, and the desk, "Oh, he's a newsman." No, I'm not. I'm the same guy I'd be if I was at the dining room table. But the wrapping makes people receive me differently. So I'm asking... How does your building look? How does your signage look? How does your website look? How do you look? Part of diligence is appearance.

There was a guy I preached for years ago. He said, "I'm believing for my church to grow." It had 11 people on Sunday morning.

I told him, "It won't grow."

He replied, "Don't speak that over me."

I responded, "Whether I speak it over you or don't speak it over you, it's not going to grow. When you walk into your church, it smells like mold and cat pee." I continued, "Your children's room is the most disgusting room I've ever been in all my travels. It's dirty. It smells dirty. It smells like old dirty diapers. If God answered your prayer and sent you 100 people next week, they'd all leave the following week."

Not everything is spiritual. Nobody cares how anointed you are if your breath knocks them off their feet. No one cares about how spiritual your church is if their children go into a dirty room that stinks. They're not going to come back. For some reason, there's always been this false equivalence among spirit-filled people that you can either be spiritual and have a dumpy church, or be seeker-sensitive with an excellent building and kick the Holy Ghost out. What happens when you do both?

The Temple in the Old Testament was an ornate building. It was not a dump. The clothes the priest ministered in had specific details for how they were made. They were beautiful. They had gems in them.

God's a God of excellence. Take what you do seriously enough to make sure it's excellent. And I'm going to tell you, it has nothing to do with how much money you have. Things that represent the kingdom should look excellent. They should look better than the rest of the world. It's a mentality, and poverty is a mentality. I don't know if unexcellence is a word, but I'm going to use it as a mentality.

Smelling nice doesn't cost money. Showering doesn't cost money. Ironing your clothes doesn't cost money. It's a mentality. Vacuuming a church doesn't cost money. Some places are nice because of how they look and smell. Four Seasons and Westin hotels have a fragrance they release into the air. It's the most beautiful fragrance. It's not overpowering. It just smells nice. We found out what they use, and we have it in the church's lobby. When you walk into the lobby of our church, you feel like you made it. It's going to be a house worthy of God's presence.

Diligence has an appearance. How does your profile picture look on social media? Here's a thought. If you're a preacher, maybe don't pick the angriest, sweatiest picture of yourself you can find. What do you think? People will look at that and think, "Who's this lunatic?" Maybe find a nice picture where you're smiling. If people are going to judge you by your outward appearance, why start with two strikes against you?

LAW SEVENTEEN

THE LAW OF CONFESSION

Confession is agreement with God. It means to speak the same thing. In the original language, the confession is to say what God's saying and line your words up with God's Word. For whatever reason, religious people do not like this doctrine. But that's why they're broke. The Law of Confession not only governs the financial anointing, the Law of Confession governs your Christianity.

> The tongue can bring death or life; those who love to talk will reap the consequences.
>
> — PROVERBS 18:21

Death and life are in what? God's hand? No. Devil's hand? Nope. Death and life are in my control…your control. Death and life are in the power of the tongue.

> For he that will love life, and see good days, let him refrain his tongue from evil, and his lips that they

> speak no guile: Let him eschew evil, and do good;
> let him seek peace, and ensue it.
>
> — 1 PETER 3:10-11 (KJV)

> For the Scriptures say,
> "If you want to enjoy life and see many happy days,
> keep your tongue from speaking evil and your lips
> from telling lies. Turn away from evil and do
> good. Search for peace, and work to maintain it."
>
> — 1 PETER 3:10-11

The Bible tells you specifically that if you want to enjoy good days, the key is to keep your lips from speaking evil. Death and life are in the power of the tongue. Confession in Western culture has a negative connotation. Confess. You confess your crime; you confess your sin to a priest. "Fess up, we know you did it." Confession is negative in Western culture, but in the Bible, it's not used the same way as in the West.

The believer is expected to know and confess four things: who I am in Christ, where I am in Christ, what I possess through Christ, and what I can do through Christ.

Number one: who I am. Most people fail this one off the bat. If you ask your average church-going Christian who they are, they will likely respond, "I'm a sinner saved by grace." This is an insane statement. How can you be a sinner and be saved? You're either one or the other.

If you ask the average Christian, "How many of you struggle with sin?" Every hand goes up. Well, what do they confess? "I'm a sinner."

Does the Bible tell you you're a sinner? No. Romans 6:1-14 says *you have dominion over sin*. 2 Corinthians 5 tells you *if any man be in Christ, he is a new creature. The old life is dead. Behold, all things have become new.* You need to get your confession correct—you are redeemed.

Number two: where I am. Where am I right now? I could say I'm in Pittsburgh, and I'm not wrong, but there's a higher reality. I'm in Pittsburgh in the physical, but where does the Bible tell you that you are as a Christian? I'm seated with Christ in heavenly places, far above all evil forces. I sit in the place of authority with Christ. Whatever doesn't have dominion over Christ, doesn't have dominion over me. That's where I'm seated—that's where all believers are.

Number three: what I possess. What do you possess as a Christian? You'll hear other preachers say "troubles…we know we all have troubles." That's misleading because it's incomplete. The Bible says I've been given all things that pertain to life and godliness; that's what I possess. The Bible says in Psalm 37 that *the righteous shall possess the land*. If I'm righteous, I'm not wrong to confess land possession, am I? When you search through the Bible, there are many things that the Bible says belong to you. I don't know why people only see the problems. "We know there's suffering." Yeah, there is, but there's many other things, too. Maybe keep reading the Bible and find them.

Number four: what I can do. What can I do through Christ? Anything? In Philippians 4:13, the Bible tells me *I can do all things through Christ who strengthens me*.

Death and life are in the power of the tongue. The Christian life, the life that a man or a woman is called to, is a life that reflects God. That's what the Bible is trying to do. It changes our carnal, fallen nature into God's divine nature and our carnal way of living into God's perfect and holy way of living.

How did God create the world? Did God think it and the earth came into being? Did we read in Genesis that God has some type of cosmic Silly Putty and he's creating the world and creating the ocean with His hands? I've heard people preach like that and say, "I believe God has on a builder's hat, right now." No. When you read the Bible, the only thing you're ever going to see God do is talk. The world we live in was framed by the words that came out of God's mouth.

God operates by speaking. Because we're created in his image, we also speak; He didn't create anything else in his image. Why can't dogs create? They can growl, they can bark. Dogs can't speak. Man was given creative power in the tongue to speak, to call things that are not as though they are.

Sadly, the average believer never taps this creative power at any time in their life. Most people just repeat what they see. "I have a tumor. It's cold outside. I don't have any money. I'm hungry." They use their mouth like a moron. They just say whatever. "It's raining out. It's getting cloudy. It's starting to get dark sooner." Their mouth is useless. They don't use their mouth to turn around their health like Jesus did for people. They just say, "I don't feel good. My eyes hurt. I can't hear as well as I used to." So, nothing changes for them. In fact, things just get worse.

Death and life are in the power of the tongue. It's up to you what flows out of your mouth. When it comes to money, the same principles apply. "We don't have a large ministry. Our ministry has never had much money. We're middle-class. Food prices are high. There's a lot of inflation right now." When you just repeat whatever's going on, the trouble continues. But you don't have to loose death out of your tongue, and you don't have to use your tongue like an idiot to just repeat whatever you're seeing. You can use your mouth to say what God said in His Word and then bring a 180-degree turnaround through your words. By your words you will be justified, and by your words you will be condemned.

If the Bible says *by His stripes, you were healed*, then I'm not wrong to say, "By His stripes, I am healed," because if I was healed, I am healed. You'll hear people say, "I don't feel healed. I don't understand how that works." I ask those people what they *do* understand; they don't understand much of anything.

Why should lack of understanding ever stop you? Could you explain it to me if I asked you how your television turns on when you hit the power button? No, you'd give me some cobbled together speech about things you heard other people say about how a TV turns on. When you get on a plane, and they tell you they're going to fly you to Denver, do you want a detailed explanation of lift and thrust from the pilot? No. You don't even see the pilot. You just take your seat and trust. But when it comes to God, and what He said, you want a detailed explanation. Until you understand everything, you won't participate. It's ridiculous when you really don't understand how much of anything works.

Why would you trust people who are below God, that they can do what they said and that things will work the way they said? And then suddenly you want God to explain Himself to you, and if it doesn't pass your mind's test, then you part company with Him? No way. If I'm going to believe anybody and I'm going to trust anybody, I'm going to trust God. God spoke it; he didn't just think it. I'm never wrong when I quote God.

I'm healed in Jesus' name. "Yeah, but you don't look any better." I'm not going by what I see. I'm going by what God said. I'm confessing the higher thing. I want you to understand that confession is not about ignoring a problem. Confession is about understanding that your tongue has been given power to change a problem. If you have a tumor, you don't ignore it, you curse it. There are things you speak for, and there are things you speak against. You can speak to a mountain and tell it to move. Your mouth can destroy bad things, and your mouth can create good things if you use it properly.

Faith and confession is not ignoring a problem, it's dealing with a problem. If you won't say it, you won't have it. If it's too big for your mouth, it's too big for your hand. If you see a home you'd like, try saying, "One day we're going to live in that house," and watch.

Any time you make a positive declaration, there will be a resistance of doubt in your mind until you learn to conquer that. I've been in a church where somebody made a statement like this: "I pray one day this church will have a million dollars in the bank, and we won't even have to have budget meetings like this. Ha, ha." They'll laugh because they can't forcefully declare it, so they have to pass it off as a joke. It's too big for their mouth and too big for their hand. They'll never have it. You have to see that the Jesus who called 153 large fish out of the sea, the Jesus that fed 5,000 men until they were full (not counting the women and children), lives in you, and you live in Him. And the same way He could call those things as though they are, the same way He could tell blind eyes to see, you are endowed with that same power. By your words will you be justified, and by your words will you be condemned.

Your words pave the highway to your destiny. A closed mouth is a closed destiny. People start feeling like they're doing good, by holding back from saying bad things. "Okay, well, I'm not going to say that kidney disease runs in my family." But what are you saying? Are you saying anything, or are you just not saying bad things? The goal is not to just avoid speaking death. The goal is to use your mouth to create life. With long life, will I satisfy you. "I have long life." You're never going to hear me say, "I know I could die at any time."

No, I'm not dying right now. I have already made up my mind. I'm going to live a long life full of blessing. That's what the Bible says, that's what I say. You hear people say, "I know the Bible says that." Yeah, you know it, but you don't believe it or speak it. "I know the Bible says that we're healed, but the truth is, right now, I'm having a lot of…" No. God is the intelligent one, and He will bring you up to a higher plane if you believe His Word and speak His Word.

> But what saith it? The word is nigh thee, even in thy mouth, and in thy heart: that is, the word of faith, which we preach;
> That if thou shalt confess with thy mouth the Lord Jesus, and shalt believe in thine heart that God hath raised him from the dead, thou shalt be saved.
> For with the heart man believeth unto righteousness; and with the mouth confession is made unto salvation.
>
> — ROMANS 10:8-10 (KJV)

There it is spelled out as plain as day. With the heart, man believeth, and with the mouth, confession is made. If you believe the Bible and the Gospel with all your heart but never make a confession with your mouth, according to Scripture, you aren't saved. You have to believe it in your heart *and* confess it with your mouth.

There is a disconnect here for many Christians because the same principle works in every other area. "I believe in healing." Yeah, but do you speak it? Or do you speak the opposite? Or do you say nothing? "I believe God wants us blessed." Yeah, do you speak it? Or do you say the opposite? Do you say things like, "I'm poor, I can't afford that. I'm having a hard time." Or are you just quiet about it?

Personally, my problem is the quiet part. I've never had a problem saying negative things, but I have had a problem not declaring the promises of God over my life and into my life. It's not enough to just believe it. There are ways to activate your faith, and one of the chief ways is by speaking.

> Thou shalt also decree a thing, and it shall be established unto thee: and the light shall shine upon thy ways.
>
> — JOB 22:28 (KJV)

Notice the order; *You decree it, and it will be established.*

Son of man, can these dry bones live again? Thou knowest. Speak to the bones and tell them to live. God didn't say, "Stand back and watch me do it." He showed him how to make dead things come to life. Speak to the bones and tell them to live. I can't think of anything crazier than speaking to bones and telling them to live. If you can speak to bones and tell them to live, you can certainly speak to your bank account, investment property, or land. Jesus said you can speak to the mountain and tell it to move.

> The next morning as they were leaving Bethany, Jesus was hungry. He noticed a fig tree in full leaf a little way off, so he went over to see if he could find any figs. But there were only leaves because it was too early in the season for fruit. Then Jesus said to the tree, "May no one ever eat your fruit again!" And the disciples heard him say it.
>
> — MARK 11:12-14

> The next morning as they passed by the fig tree he had cursed, the disciples noticed it had withered from the roots up. Peter remembered what Jesus had said to the tree on the previous day and exclaimed, "Look, Rabbi! The fig tree you cursed has withered and died!"
>
> — MARK 11:20-21

I want you to notice that when Jesus cursed that tree, they didn't see anything happen right away. But then, in the morning, they saw it had dried up from the roots. That's why you don't go by sight. With sight, you only see the tree bark and leaves, but God's Word declared through your mouth goes to the root. Did Jesus say, "No one will ever eat fruit from you again. Oh, it still looks the same. Well. I guess I took that doctrine too far." No. *In the morning, as they passed by, they saw the fig tree dried up by the roots. And Peter calling to remembrance, saith unto him, Master, behold the fig tree which thou cursedst is withered away. Jesus answering saith unto them, Have faith in God.*

There is no faith without confession. With the heart man believeth, with the mouth confession is made. Faith and confession are tied together eternally.

> For verily I say unto you, That whosoever shall say unto this mountain, Be thou removed, and be thou cast into the sea; and shall not doubt in his heart, but shall believe that those things which he saith shall come to pass; he shall have whatsoever he saith.
>
> — MARK 11:23 (KJV)

Mark 11:23 mentions what you *believe* only once, and you *speak* three times. Could it be that Jesus mentioned what you speak three times and what you believe, one time because man has a three times harder job with their confession than they do their believing? It's possible. The tongue is impossible to control outside of the Holy Ghost. No man can tame it. James said it sets people's lives on fire and it's set on fire by Hell itself. Jesus, in this great passage on faith, dealt with what you say three times, and only mentioned "believe" one time.

What do most Christians say? "I don't know why it's not happening. I believe." Well, did you just hear yourself? You believe, and you said, "I don't know why it's not happening." That's not a faith confession. That's unbelief. "I don't know why things aren't working out."

If I've ever come to your church, you've noticed I come about 25 minutes late. I try to miss the opening part of the service for many reasons. One of the reasons is that at most churches, I either feel like quitting the ministry or rebuking everything that was sung by the time worship is over. There used to be another hellish song everybody sang where the chorus says, "He gives and takes away." Where are you getting that from? How much crack do you smoke before you pick your worship songs? "Well, the Bible says he gives and takes away." Yeah, Job said it, and he got rebuked for it at the end of the book, because God never took one thing away from Job. The Devil did, and God gave it back.

People think they have faith, but their confession tells you otherwise. When some pastors ask, "How many of us are going through a hard time right now?" You're not going to get me to lift my hand. I don't see myself as going through a hard time. I see myself as blessed and highly favored. You can't do both. Attacks are real, and God said *when your enemy attacks you from one direction, I'll make him run from you in seven directions.* You don't even have to concern yourself with it. He didn't even say you had to pray. *You abide in the shadow of the Almighty, and I'll take care of your enemies. Vengeance is mine, saith the Lord. I will repay.* If you're going to get on the "prosperity bus," you must get off the "struggle bus." You can't ride both buses.

When COVID hit, and they said we can't gather with more than 10 people at a time, in the natural, that's not going to bode well for somebody like me. I gather crowds. That heavily affects me if I'm not allowed to preach to crowds of people. Secondly, if they're shutting everybody's business down, and the Dow Jones has dropped about 50%, and unemployment is supposed to go to 40%, I know the first area where people cut back is charitable giving. You're not going to give to help feed other people if you can't feed your own family. Right?

I'll be honest with you, I was concerned. But I'm going to give you a tip that'll change your life; if doubt ever comes into your head, don't let it go down the elevator and come out of your mouth because it doesn't say, "Death and life are in the power of your thoughts." It says *death and life are in the power of the tongue.* You can't stop a bird from flying over your head, but you can stop a bird from building a nest in your hair.

The Bible says *casting down every thought and vain imagination that would exalt itself against God*, which tells you, anybody will have thoughts come that are contrary to the Word of God. That's not a sin. When Jesus the Messiah was in the wilderness and Satan came and said: *Bow down to me, and I'll give you the wealth and kingdoms of this world, for they're mine to give to whomever I choose, for they've been delivered unto me*, and Jesus responded to him. For Jesus to respond to what Satan said, what did Jesus have to do? He heard what Satan said, His mind had to process what Satan said to come up with a response. If thinking something wrong was a sin, then Jesus sinned, but Jesus never sinned.

Having a wrong thought is not a sin. You have the power to cast that thought down, and how do you do it? What did Jesus do? Jesus didn't just go, "You go ahead and keep speaking, Satan. I'm not going to believe it." No, He spoke the opposite of what Satan said; Jesus spoke from the Word of God. Notice how powerful scriptural confession is. Satan never argued with Christ's scriptural confession, instead, he changed the subject. Satan will not argue with what's written. If you know the Word and speak the Word, Satan has nothing to say. It's a sword that cuts him down. How did Jesus repel Lucifer himself? By speaking the Word. He never said, "I rebuke you, Satan." He didn't pray in speed tongues. "It is written, it is written, it is written."

I think of how entirely different my world would be right now if I had said in March 2020, "Guys, this is going to be a hard year. I don't know how we're going to make it or if we're going to make it." Can you imagine? Let me ask you a question: How did two different ministries go through the same pandemic, one lays off two thirds of their workers and loses their property, the other one buys more property, hires more staff, and gives everyone raises? Death and life are in the power of the tongue. In my head, I thought it would take a miracle for us to have the same income in 2020 as we had in 2019. I thought if we only have a 20% regression, that'll be a miracle. Instead, it almost doubled. During the same pandemic, we broke the previous year's all-time high in revenue, and that happened just over halfway through the year. We've given one million dollars to other ministers and ministries in the last nine months. This was all in the midst of a pandemic.

Did I go through a different pandemic than other ministries did? No. It's your response to the storm. You don't wait for storms to pass, instead you speak to the storm. You can speak to storms, you can speak to fig trees, you can speak to dry bones. You can speak to mountains. You can speak to debt. You can speak to insufficiency. You can speak to lack. When Jesus told us we can speak to a mountain, he wasn't trying to get us to move Pike's Peak to Idaho. You can speak to something that in the natural is large, insurmountable, and immovable and command it to move, and it will obey your command. Not it "might" obey your command. It will obey your command.

I felt the Lord speak two things in March of 2020; "Son, if you do what I tell you to do, you will have the best year you've ever had." But then God didn't just let me believe it, He said to me, "Call your staff in tomorrow and tell them that no one will be laid off during this pandemic. No one will have their pay decreased." That's how you know there's power in speaking. I didn't have a problem believing what I heard God say on the inside of me, because then it's just me, you know? If I was wrong, no one knows. But to call a bunch of people in a room and say, "Hey, listen. I know you're hearing the stock market's tanking. Unemployment's going to go up to 40%. All businesses are shut down. But I just wanted to call you in to tell you, relax, because we're going to have the best year we've ever had, nobody's going to get fired, and no one will have their pay decreased." *Thou shalt decree a thing and it shall be established,* which is exactly what happened.

Faith will work in your heart while you still have doubt in your head. Your mind is carnal. If you have a second voice in your head while you're speaking that says, "I don't know if that's going to work," that's normal. It won't stop faith from working, as long as you don't let the doubt come out of your mouth. But if you let it come out of your mouth, it'll ruin everything.

"Father, we believe you can heal Mary Johnson. Though she's sick and the doctors have given her up to die, you're the God who parted the Red Sea. We know there's nothing you can't do. We speak healing to her right now. But even if it is not your will, we understand. In Jesus' name." What was with the last part? You were doing really good on one track, and then you grabbed the wheel and made an illegal lane change into the lane of doubt and unbelief. That's how they prayed for the sick when I was growing up in church, and I never saw one person get a miracle in 18 years from church prayer. I never saw anybody come off the sick list unless a doctor treated them because every prayer had an unbelief clause at the end of the contract. What do you mean even if it's not His will? He said He'd answer your prayer.

You must believe in your heart and confess with your mouth. You have what you say, and you can't speak with a forked tongue. Imagine if I'd have called my staff back a week later and said, "Now, guys, I know I told you no one's going to get their pay decreased, but bear in mind that this is getting worse than I expected, so anything can happen." A double-minded man is unstable in all his ways. Let not that man expect to receive anything from the Lord.

> If any of you lack wisdom, let him ask of God, that giveth to all men liberally, and upbraideth not; and it shall be given him.
> But let him ask in faith, nothing wavering. For he that wavereth is like a wave of the sea driven with the wind and tossed.
> For let not that man think that he shall receive any thing of the Lord.
> A double minded man is unstable in all his ways.
>
> — JAMES 1:5-8 (KJV)

Why are most Christians unstable? Because they're double-minded. "I believe God's a healer, but at the same time, I believe we all struggle." Their main confession is double-minded. "I'm a sinner saved by grace." How much more double-minded can you get than that? This is the most insane sentence you could read; "I'm a sinner saved." How can you be a sinner who's saved? You're either one or the other. Most people's Christianity is built on a double-minded confession. "I know He's perfect, but how many of you know we're nothing?" Then you're double-minded and unstable in all your ways. What happens if you switch it and instead say, "I'm the righteousness of God in Christ. I'm seated with Christ in heavenly places. I possess all things that pertain to life and godliness."

What I confess, I possess. You confess sin, you'll have sin. You confess sickness, you'll have sickness. If you confess poverty and insufficiency and lack, you'll have all three. What you confess, you possess. What you have is what you say. If someone says, "We have a small ministry," I know why. If someone says, "We're not really seeing any people come to our church," I understand the root of the problem; it's that little red muscle in your mouth. What if, instead, you said, "Father, I thank you for the supernatural increase in our church this month. I thank you that we'll see more visitors come to Jesus Christ this month than we've ever seen in the history of our ministry." What if you start talking like that?

If Jesus said, "I've come that you might have life and have it more abundantly," then why do people think it's normal to say, "How many of you are struggling; lift your hand"? What would happen if you started to think it's normal to have abundance? How many of you live with more than enough money to do what God called you to do and enjoy life with your family? That's what abundant life means. How long does it take to get to abundant life? 10 years? I'm not saying this to be mean. I'm saying it to prick you because if you're ever going to make a change, you've got to snap out of thinking certain things are normal.

If you've been a Christian for 20 years and you've not come into abundant life, something's wrong because Jesus said: *I've come that you might have life and have it more abundantly.* How many 20-year periods are you going to let go by? You only get four, maybe five. You don't have 10 and 20 years to play around. I just crested into my 40s. This 20-year period from 40 to 60 is an extremely important 20 years. It determines whether I'll be irrelevant at 60 or have an international voice at 60. You don't play around. "I'm just waiting on God." What are you waiting for? What is left for Him to do that hasn't been made available to you through His Word? You don't wait for it to fall in your lap, you believe it and speak it into being.

Confession brings possession. What you don't fight for, you'll never have. Is it wrong to say that the law of confession can work in the financial realm? Let me ask you a question: If it was wrong, wouldn't they have to rip 1 Kings 17 out of the Bible? If somebody criticized this message and said, "You can't say that speaking brings prosperity." Then I'd ask them to explain 1 Kings 17 to me.

> For thus saith the Lord God of Israel, The barrel of meal shall not waste, neither shall the cruse of oil fail, until the day that the Lord sendeth rain upon the earth.
>
> — 1 KINGS 17:14 (KJV)

Did it happen? Yeah. Did Elijah lay hands on it? No. Elijah spoke a prophetic word about financial increase. Unless you can get God to agree to smite that out of His Word, it's there whether you like it or not. What about 2 Kings 7? There was a national famine. How did

Elisha solve it? Did he make some phone calls? Did he try to get some food distributors together that could get food into the country? No. Elisha said: *By this time tomorrow, there'll be an overabundance of food.* And the king's assistant said: *That couldn't happen even if the Lord opened the windows of heaven!* Elisha said: *You'll see it with your eyes, but you won't taste it,* and both words came true. The food came, and the guy died after seeing it come in. Unbelief carries a cost; faith carries a reward.

How did Peter's boat get filled up with fish? Did Jesus jump in the water and start gathering up fish and bringing them into his boat? Jesus said: *Cast your net, go out into the deep, cast your net down, and you'll catch some fish.* Peter responded with: *At thy word I'll do it.* So, he did as Jesus said, and the nets began to tear, and the boats began to sink, for the catch of fish was so great. What about when Jesus and Peter needed to pay their taxes? What did Jesus do? Start making investments? Go and catch a fish. The first fish you catch, there'll be a gold coin in its mouth with enough to pay your taxes and my taxes. I don't read where Jesus said, "I don't know how we're going to pay our taxes." No, instead he spoke.

> "I promise you what I promised Moses: 'Wherever you set foot, you will be on land I have given you—'"
>
> — JOSHUA 1:3

Notice the scripture does not say, wherever the sole of your foot shall tread, I'll *give* you the land. It says: *Wherever the sole of your foot will tread, you'll be on land that I've already given you.* That's a big difference. It's already yours when you put your feet on it.

The main difference between the old covenant and the new covenant is that in the old covenant, they did things physically. In the new covenant, it's handled in the spirit. For example, in the Old Testament, if you have demonically inspired enemies to keep the Israelites out of the Promised Land, you killed them. In the new covenant, when you have demonically inspired enemies, you don't see Paul kill a sorcerer. You don't see the church kill King Agrippa. You see them speak, and then it's carried out in the spirit.

In the Old Covenant, if they wanted to take land, they had to put their feet on it. They did things physically. In the new covenant, we take care of it spiritually. The Bible shows you that the vehicle for taking care of things is your words. Your words in the new covenant are your feet that touch the land that God has already given you. You're not trying to get Him to give you anything. All things that pertain to life and godliness have already been provided.

We put our feet and words on what He has already said is ours. Were the Israelites already living in their Promised Land? No. Had God already given it to them? Yes. What did they have to do to actuate it? They had to put their feet on what God had already given them.

Has God already made riches and abundance yours? More than enough yours? Yes. Are you living in it? Some are, some aren't. But for those who aren't, you don't look at it as something out of your reach to grasp. It's already yours; now put your feet on it, which is your mouth in the new covenant. Put your mouth on it. "Blessing belongs to me. I will lay up an inheritance for my children's children. The righteous shall possess the land." These are not things I'm trying to get God to do, He's already done it. Just like He already turned Canaan over to them, though there were other people living in it. The way you take the giants off of your Promised Land is by putting your words on your Promised Land.

Some things you must never confess. "I'm broke. I can't afford that. We're not rich. I don't have enough money. We can't afford to live in a house like that. I can't afford a car. I don't have enough money to fly." Never confess lack. But remember, it's not enough just to shut the spigot of doubt off from coming out of your mouth. That just keeps your mouth inactive. What can you confess? What do you have scriptural grounds to confess? And specifically, what do you have scriptural grounds to confess in the realm of prosperity? Houses, land, all needs provided, more than enough equipment and clothing. It's all in the Bible, but it won't do you any good until you put your feet on the land. Line your mouth up with God's Word.

> This book of the law shall not depart out of thy mouth; but thou shalt meditate therein day and night, that thou mayest observe to do according to all that is written therein: for then thou shalt make thy way prosperous, and then thou shalt have good success.
>
> — JOSHUA 1:8 (KJV)

Joshua 1:8 doesn't say this book of the law shall never depart from your mind, though it talks about meditating on it day and night. Interestingly, it doesn't say this book of the law shall never depart from your heart. It says: *This book of the law shall not depart from your mouth.*

Speak it. If you don't say it, you'll never have it. This book of the law must never depart from your mouth. When you're in your vehicle by yourself, turn the radio off and say some things. It's just you in there anyway. Death and life are in the power of the tongue, and the law of confession is something you can put to work today for your benefit, particularly for your financial benefit.

LAW EIGHTEEN

THE LAW OF THANKSGIVING AND PRAISE

The Law of Thanksgiving and Praise; there's a connection between praise and prosperity.

> May God be merciful and bless us. May His face smile with favor on us. May your ways be known throughout the earth, your saving power among people everywhere. May the nations praise you, O God. Yes, may all the nations praise you. Let the whole world sing for joy, because you govern the nations with justice and guide the people of the whole world.
>
> — PSALM 67:1-4

It's amazing how the above Scripture declares the will of God—that all nations would praise Him. On Sundays, all nations do praise Him. This started in an upper room in the book of Acts. Now in every nation of the world, they're singing at 9:00 AM, 10:00 AM, 11:00 AM unto God. Pretty amazing; it's the will of God.

Number one, when someone doesn't thank you, you're constrained from doing anything further for them. If you do something for someone and there's no gratitude, there's very little motivation to help them again. You don't have to be a vindictive person, you don't necessarily regret doing what you did, and you don't bring it up to them, but you're done doing anything to help that person. I could tell you some examples of this in my own life, but I'll move on. There's nothing worse than someone who feels entitled to something and thinks you should have done more. Especially when you didn't have to do anything in the first place. True or false?

I get irritated thinking about people feeling entitled to something you do for them. In my opinion, that's why many, many traveling ministries stay poor. They have no appreciation for what's done for them. It's always about what more should have been done.

"You should have seen the hotel this church put me in." Why didn't you check out? I know why, because you're a cheapskate.

"You should have seen the low offering they gave me." Well, maybe your service sucked, and people didn't feel like giving. Never any gratitude. When someone doesn't thank you, you're constrained from doing anything further, and scripturally this also applies to God.

Until you thank God for the last thing, you're disqualified from receiving anything else. Until you thank God for the last thing, you'll never receive the next thing.

Number two, the only thing God can't do is praise Himself. If you read any Catholic Catechism book and ask, "What is the purpose of men?" They have the same answer because it's the correct scriptural answer. The purpose of man is to give thanks and praise to God. You were created to give God what He's unable to give Himself, thanksgiving and praise. God won't allow anybody into His presence without thanksgiving in their hearts and praise in their mouths. That's the entry code to get in.

In James 1, the Bible says that *your prayers aren't answered because you ask amiss*; you don't pray correctly. There are technicalities to prayer. We've done whole teachings on this. You have to go to the Father or it doesn't work. You have to go in the name of Jesus, or it doesn't work. You have to pray in faith, doubting nothing, or it doesn't work.

Number three; you can't praise amiss. You can't praise incorrectly. It's impossible to miss when you express gratitude, praise, and thanksgiving to God.

When teaching the 20 laws that govern the financial anointing, people say things like, "Tell me something I can actually do that will affect my money." So, **number four**, praise affects the physical realm. If you think this is just a theoretical "pie in the sky" talk that won't have bearing on your financial situation, there are instances in the Bible you need to see. I'll give you one in particular. Paul and Silas prayed, but you don't read about anything happening when they prayed. They were singing praises to God, and the prisoners heard them in loud vocal praise. They weren't in a sheetrock cell. They were in a Roman stone dungeon. The other prisoners could hear them. Suddenly there was an earthquake. The chains fell off every prisoner, and every prison door opened. What provoked that? Praise. Don't tell me that praise doesn't have an effect. If praise can knock off iron chains, praise can knock off invisible chains. If praise can open actual prison doors, praise can open invisible prison doors. Praise affects the physical realm.

Number five, complaining causes what you have to diminish. You can read the story of the Israelites in the wilderness. When they complained about what they were lacking, it attracted vipers to bite them, and they died. They were sad, and then they were dead. Complaining causes a bad situation to get worse. Complaining attracts a curse, just like praise attracts a blessing. In the book of Numbers, serpents were drawn to the complainers. God regarded their complaining as an evil thing. Complaining engenders curses. It's like a magnet to trouble. Complaining will never improve your life, so you have to shut the door to complaining.

Number six, just like complaining diminishes, thanksgiving multiplies. And until thanks has been given, nothing multiplies. Thanksgiving engenders multiplication. Jesus has 5,000 men to feed, not counting women and children. They give Him a little boy's lunch, five loaves of bread, and two fishes. What does Jesus say? "What am I supposed to do with this?" No, He blessed it and thanked God for it. And then the multiplication began. Nothing multiplies until you give thanks.

Can you imagine having 15,000 people to feed and somebody gives you five pieces of bread and two fish? And you go, "Wow, thank you God. You've provided". People start asking, "Are you okay in the head? This is good enough to feed one little boy, not 15,000." It seems insane to thank God, but when you thank God for what you have, it actually causes an increase. Praising God causes the earth to yield its harvest.

> May the nations praise you, O God. Yes, may all the
> nations praise you. Then the earth will yield its
> harvests, and God, our God, will richly bless us.
>
> — PSALM 67:5-6

When I was preparing this message, I was thinking back to when I was making maybe $300 every two weeks when I first started my ministry. Then when I got married, Adalis traveled with me. She didn't receive a salary. I worked for another ministry, and then I was given around $30K a year. That was our only income as a couple. Needless to say, there were many times when we checked our bank account. We had times when the bank account had $26 left, and we weren't getting paid for another eight days. I wasn't reflecting on this to complain. I'm saying it doesn't make any sense because we always ate well. I probably ate better than I do now because I don't feel like going to restaurants anymore. We ate at places where we had no business eating. That's how I lived back then, and we never hit bottom. We never complained, never had reason to complain. Of course, if you're a complainer, you can always find a reason to complain.

Essentially, if you tithe, give seed above the tithe, and stay in gratitude and thanksgiving with your mouth, you go up, you can't hit bottom. I've tried very, very hard. Let me tell you something. If what I'm teaching you doesn't work, you would know because I would be on a park bench under a blanket. There's nothing you could point to in my life or in our ministry that was done by wise financial management. We just give and give and give and give and give. I meet people on the road often, and we connect with people who mention we paid for the apartment they're living in. I don't remember helping them; I just did it and forgot. So, just fling seed around every time you feel led, and you'll never hit bottom. Give in thanks.

Thank you, Jesus. Thank you for taking me further. Thank you for taking me higher. What an awesome God you are.

Keep giving, keep thanking. There's a strong correlation between your praise and your prosperity.

No wonder every demon-possessed tyrant during COVID told churches to stop singing. If the Devil can shut up your praise, he can shut up your harvest. A "Thanksgiver" never goes backward. Showing genuine gratitude to God and people who have blessed you is one of the highest keys to prosperity. And I don't mean thanking people, hoping they do another thing for you. I'm talking about expressing genuine thanks for what they've done.

Many, many preachers feel entitled that people should have to give them money. "The Bible says to tithe." Yeah, but it doesn't say anything about tithing to you. "The Bible says you're to give offerings." It doesn't say anything about your ministry in there. When people choose your soil for their sowing, that should invoke gratitude to God. If I know someone has money, I've never said, "You know that person there? They make six figures. They've never given more than $50 in one of my offerings." Number one, I don't count the offering, so I wouldn't know. Number two, it's theirs to give or not to give. No one owes me money because they have money, and I'm in the ministry.

There should be genuine gratitude to God in the heart of any minister. Point A, for the Holy Spirit speaking to them to give to you, you should be thankful to God. And B, for them being obedient. There should be a genuine gratitude in a minister for a vessel he's used. "Thank you. I know you didn't have to do that. God will bless you, but I'm saying thank you." It seems like people either go to one extreme or the other. They either don't have gratitude toward people God uses. Or if God uses a vessel to bless them, they make that person into their god. "Do you see that guy? He's a doctor. He comes to our church. He has given thousands of dollars to this church. I don't know what our ministry would do without him." And God says, "Hey, I'll let you find out. I'll let you find out what your ministry will do without me since you have him now, and you're just praising him to everyone."

Don't fall into a ditch on either side of the road. The ditch of ingratitude or the other ditch, singing praises of the person who helped you. Praise is reserved for God. Thank people but remember that God is your source. Then you never have to be held captive by anybody.

If you don't understand the laws of prosperity, if you don't understand that God is your source, the Devil will manipulate you with money for the rest of your life. But if you learn that God is your source, no one can ever manipulate you with money.

The manipulation may come from a member of your church saying, "As you know, we're the largest tithers in this church. We did not like the guest speaker that you just had in. So, if he comes back, I will probably look for another church."

"I just want to tell you very clearly; you are free to go to another church anytime you'd like." The God that sent that tither to your church will send more people to your church. God's not held hostage by givers.

If you understand that God is your source, no one can ever manipulate you with money. I don't see Elijah pulling out charts and graphs for the ravens about what he's planning to do in his ministry, and then they agree to give him bread and meat. There's another flow you can get into. It's called the financial anointing, and it takes you out of the control of men.

Number 7, angels attend to our prayers. This is powerful. In Daniel 10, the Bible says that when Daniel fasted and prayed, an angel was sent to give him his answer. An angel was loosed from that prayer. In Acts 12,

Peter was put in prison, and the church began to pray very earnestly for him. An angel was sent to break him out. The Bible says in Psalm 22: *God abides in the praises of His people.* Angels attend to our prayers; God attends to our praise. Angels go to work for our prayers. God personally visits the person who gives praise and thanksgiving.

The church prayed for Peter. An angel came and broke him out of prison. Paul sang praises, and there was an earthquake, and the doors broke open. That didn't happen with Peter. With Peter, an angel came and let him out. Paul, the one door opened for him, and his chains fell off. Who do you think caused the earthquake when they began to sing? Angels attend to your prayers; God visits the praiser, and God attends to your praise.

For many years, I had no clue about the things I just taught you from the Bible. And I'm going to tell you a story about how God broke us out of poverty in 2015 and brought Adalis and me into a place of prosperity by our praise.

I'd probably had less than ten times in my life when people gave me $100. I was not content with where I was at. I knew what God had shown me when He called me into the ministry, so I knew there must be a way to get there. I was tired of treading water. So, I went on a fast. I had sown financially, and I'd given all I could give. We had no mailing list. No one at that time had partnered with us.

One day my wife got the mail, which used to be nothing but bills—usually ones we forgot to pay the month before. At the time, I was driving a car that hadn't been registered in two years. I couldn't get it registered because the back end was smashed in, and I didn't have enough money to fix it. So, my wife checks the mail and discovers somebody had written us a check for $1,000. I had never even heard of that. I don't believe my bank account had ever been over a thousand dollars in my life.

When that came in, I was so amazed because there's no way people could have been aware of our needs. We weren't sending newsletters out or asking for help. I knew God had placed it on someone's heart to do that. I became so overwhelmed with love for God, that I started dancing in my little 800 square-foot cockroach-infested apartment in Virginia Beach. I was raised in a Pentecostal church in a preacher's home; we weren't allowed to dance. I wasn't allowed to go to dances, and we weren't allowed to dance in church either—they didn't even play music you could dance to. I didn't know any dance moves, but I got so overwhelmed that I wanted to dance before God. So, I danced. I knew a move from Junkyard Dog, so I did that along with a couple other terrible moves. It must have looked like I was having a slow-motion seizure, but I did my best.

My wife saw me dancing from the other room. I was caught up in thanking God. But when I looked at her, she was laughing so hard she was completely doubled over. I said, "What are you laughing at? You dance too. God did this for us." And so, she reluctantly danced. We were just newlyweds, and she still wasn't comfortable doing something like that in front of me. So, she danced a little. Seeing her laughing gave me an idea. I'd never read Psalm 67 and understood it like I'm going to teach it now, but I thought maybe if this is as amusing to God as it is to my wife, He'll give me checks just to watch me dance. I went into my bedroom and shut the door behind me. I said, "God, if you enjoyed that dance, I'll tell you what... Anytime you give me a check, I will dance for you. And I'll dance in proportion to how big the check is. So, if somebody gives me a check for like $7, I'll give you a little dance. But if it's $10,000 I'll dance till I'm out of energy." That was the deal I made; even as I said it, I thought it was insane.

We were about to go to the next meeting at a church in St. Mary's, West Virginia that seated 25 people. It was the kind of church where I was believing God for just enough gas money to get home. My wife said, "Would you like to check the mail before we leave?" No, because mail was always bad news. But she was insistent that we check the mail. She comes back from the mailbox, and there's a torn open letter she throws onto my lap. Anytime she ever brought mail to me, I figured it was the IRS or something big because she usually handled the small stuff. But there was a check for $1,700 from another person. I thought, "It's working!" I immediately flung the car door open, jumped out in the parking lot, and started to dance as hard as I could. And I'll tell you, I had room in every direction. Mothers were stirring their children up, "Don't look at that man, don't make eye contact with him. Just come with me. Don't pay any attention to him." I was spinning and dancing. And then I sat back into the car. I said, "Look, look what God's doing."

We go to the church at St. Mary's West Virginia that Sunday. This old farmer started talking to my wife and said, would you like to come over to our house and shoot guns? That's how people make small talk in West Virginia. Instead of having you over for dinner, you just come and shoot things for fun. We go there and shoot. When it was time to leave, this old guy says, "Before you go, I want to give you an envelope." He gave it to me, but he didn't tell me what was in it. Once I held it, I felt it was thick. I'd gotten ones like this before where somebody wrote their prophetic dream on 12 pages, small print on both sides. So, I said thank you. I wanted to see what was in it, but I didn't want to open it in front of him.

As soon as we got out of his driveway, I drove slowly and ripped it open while driving. I could feel that it wasn't notebook paper, it was paper bills. I thought it was probably twenties or fives; something like that. So, I start counting out with my thumbs, I couldn't believe it—$3,600. So, I count again, $3,600. My wife asks, what is it? I just took the wad of money and threw it on her lap without saying anything.

And she said, "Pull the car over." She jumped out and started dancing. And I got out beside her, and I started dancing.

From never having anybody give us a thousand dollars, we had 27 people give us money in the next three months, at least $1,000 or more. Everywhere we went it happened. I have never stopped dancing or praising since. Let me tell you something. The Bible says to put on the garment of praise and sow the spirit of happiness. The enemy's work is to surround you with people who say "It's hard you know, it's hard when you're starting out in ministry. It's hard pastoring." The Devil wants you to start saying that junk. When you loose those words, it's like releasing death; it cuts off your provision.

But if you say "No, Devil, I'm not saying that; I will say the opposite. *I will bless the Lord at all times, His praise shall continually be in my mouth. Bless the Lord I tell my soul and forget not all of His benefits. Who heals all my diseases and forgives my sin. He ransoms me from death. He fills my life with good things. My cup runneth over. Surely goodness and mercy will follow me all the days of my life*," you shall not be defeated. You won't give up and quit.

The Bible says that there was a wall when the Israelites were instructed to take Jericho. Nobody comes into the promise God has for them uncontested. There was a wall to keep them out that nobody had ever been able to breach. God didn't say, "When that wall falls, praise me." He said, "If you shout first, you're not going to need to do the rest." Now think of this. That wall was so wide that six chariots could run across it simultaneously. So even if the wall collapsed, it was still a wall. You saw when the twin towers fell, you couldn't walk over it. So, it wasn't enough for the wall to just collapse.

It's like C4 and a detonator; one without the other is no good. You can shout all you want. If you don't give, nothing works. But when you plant your seed and then praise. If you consecrate time and praise—

you should try sometime to fast and praise—you can't come out depressed and praise. Angels attend to our prayers, but God attends to our praise. He abides in the praises of his people. And when God comes down, every wall doesn't just collapse. The Bible says it fell flat so that they could go right into the city. In the name of Jesus, when we shout, every wall that has kept you out of the land God said is yours, it falls flat in the name of Jesus.

That whole story is true. Go write your own story. God will be very good to you. If you always remember that everything came from His hand, prove it by returning things. Even the tithe is a reminder, "By the way God, I'm still very clear on who my source is." You wouldn't miss bank payments. Why? You know they're the source of your house if you have a mortgage—if you cut out on the deal, there will be trouble. In the same way, don't cut out on continual thanksgiving to God.

LAW NINETEEN

THE MILLIONAIRE LAW

This is The Millionaire Law because whatever your dream is, if it's going to be any kind of dream at all, it will not require a million dollars—it's going to require *millions* of dollars. What I'm teaching in this chapter is an understanding you must have, or none of the other things will work. You've got to ask yourself what it takes to become a millionaire. I'm talking mathematically; I'm not talking about confession, I'm not talking faith. Mathematically, what does it take to start generating a million dollars? If the Lord has given you a business dream, if the Lord's given you a dream in the realm of art, if the Lord's given you a dream in the realm of entertainment, it won't even get off the ground without cresting a million dollars.

My Uncle Ted, a minister, posted a picture of himself with Rodney Howard-Browne, as a tribute to Dr. Rodney. With the picture, he wrote, "He is a true prophet of God and loved by me. Arrested for having church. Prophetically wrote about 2020 and was accused of conspiracy theories until it came to pass. A soul winner for the cause of Christ. May the Lord bless him and Adonica greatly."

A lady tweeted back and said, "He's a megachurch." First of all, he's not a megachurch; he's a human being who pastors what she considers a megachurch. She continues, "He's a megachurch, and like Osteen, and the Grahams, and all the other mega-millionaire pastors, he's there to receive us." I think she means to receive from us. She goes on, "No pastor should be worth millions. And I know a lot of dirt on these megachurches." Notice how angry she was that a pastor had millions of dollars. If anything, you'd think a Christian would post something online saying, "It irritates me that pornographers have millions of dollars. It irritates me that Jeffrey Epstein could, through human trafficking, have his own private island. It bothers me that casinos make millions of dollars." But she didn't say that, did she? She said, "No pastor should ever have millions of dollars." You must be a special kind of stupid to think like that, especially as a believer. Of all the things you could be upset about, you're upset that a leader in your own faith is doing well financially?

I bring this up to deal with the one statement she made when she said that no pastor should be worth millions. I don't want to deal with the fact that no pastor should be worth millions. I want the deal with the small-mindedness shared by that lady and many others. I'm not saying this to be insulting, but you may even think this way without realizing it.

I'll give you an example. When I was flying on a ministry trip to preach in another nation, one of the other pastors and I had business class tickets. Eight other ministers were coming on the trip, which I was unaware of, and they all had tickets for seating in coach. As I stated before, I didn't know any of the other ministers coming on the trip. While we were in line, these other ministers said to the pastor who I knew, "Oh, it must be nice to fly in business class. How were you able to do that?" Then they made snide jokes. "It must be nice to be rich."

I'm reminded of Lester Sumrall's story about an experience that changed his life. When he met Robert A. Brown, and his wife, Marie Brown, they had the largest church in America at the time. I think there were about 3,000 church members during a time when 200 people were considered a megachurch. Robert Brown had to speak at a conference in California. This was in the 1920s; there weren't flights back then, so he took the transcontinental railroad from New York to California. I think it took five days.

When Robert A. Brown got off the train, Lester Sumrall, who was also speaking at the conference, also got off, but he was all hunched over with wrinkled clothing. He says to Brown, "Man, I can't wait to sleep. But we have a service in a couple of hours. I'm exhausted from that train ride. You must be exhausted too."

Brown said, "No. I got a suite in the berth."

You could have a regular seat where you just sit upright in a seat for five days, or you could rent a little room. There's a bath, a bed, and your own little private area.

After saying he rented a room in the berth, Sumrall said, "You rented a room in the berth? How dare you spend the Lord's money like that?"

Robert Brown calmly replied, "Oh, the Lord doesn't mind. He'd rather have me ready to preach than ready to sleep."

Half of this is good theology, and the other half is the fact that Brown's Irish. When you're Irish you know how to cut people down in a quick phrase. Since Lester Sumrall just said he had to preach in a couple hours but would rather go sleep, he already hung himself by his words.

Robert Brown continued, "I'm fresh as a daisy. I'm ready to do what God's called me to do. You're the one that looks like you got dragged in. You said with your own mouth, you're not ready to preach." You can see there are two distinct mentalities.

FAITH IS A UNIVERSAL CURRENCY

Faith is a universal currency that works anywhere in the world. You need to know this; otherwise, a lot of international people will immediately write themselves off. Preachers in India think they need American preachers to bless them. "You know, the economy's very bad here, and our currency's very weak." That's a false mentality. Are the wealthiest ministries in the world in America, are they in Europe, or are they in West Africa? They're in West Africa. So obviously, the nation that you're in and its economy have zero bearing on God's ability to bless you.

Faith is a universal currency that works in any nation. It'll work in China. It'll work in North Korea. It'll work in Iran. You can't see yourself as a disadvantaged person.

ONE MILLION DOLLARS IS ATTAINABLE FOR ME

A million dollars immediately becomes $700,000 after the government takes its cut. You can't talk about a million dollars like it's 1840, or even 1980. Back then, a million dollars was still an amount of money that, if you had it, you could quit your job and just retire. You might only be able to do that now if you lived frugally off the interest. However, thanks to inflation and the insane people running the Federal Reserve System, one million dollars is no longer something unattainable or even difficult to attain. As long as you see something as unattainable, you'll never have it.

For example, if you are an average-looking male with an average body, and somebody shows you a chiseled male movie star with six-pack abs, you say, "Man, I could never… How does somebody even look like that?" You'll never look like that. If you think it's unattainable, you'll never have that body.

If somebody tells you, "Listen, if you give me 90 minutes every day, I can have you looking like that, or close to that, in about eight months if you'll eat and train like I tell you." Then it takes the mystery out of it. They start telling you what to eat and drink and how to exercise properly. Suddenly, you have a path to achieving something that once seemed completely unattainable. It's the same in the realm of money. If a million dollars is something you chuckle about or something you talk about as a fictitious number, you'll never have it.

You cannot tell me an amount of money you inherited or earned that will unsettle or upset me. The more you have, the happier I will be. The woman I told you about earlier said, "He's like the Osteens or the Grahams." What did Joel Osteen ever do? Where's the anger towards Joel Osteen coming from? If he earned his money illegally, then put him in jail—but he didn't. What story do you think their finances will tell? …that a man who hasn't taken a salary from his church for 20 years is a multi-millionaire because it came through other streams. She also brought up Billy and Franklin Graham. What did they ever do? What did they ever do for you to say that they shouldn't have millions?

Right now, there's a guy on the street in Philadelphia asking if anybody has money for sandwiches and another guy in Philadelphia driving a Bentley. There are two types of people. The stupid person trained in public school and university, brainwashed to see both the begging man and the man with the Bentley, and say, "That's not fair; society is unjust."

Then the wise person will say, "Those two men have made very different choices in life." You might be living in a fantasy world if you think the begging man didn't make any poor choices—a tragedy may be responsible for him living on the street. There's a tiny percentage chance that is true.

If you talk to both guys, you'll find that one decided to invest his money in real estate, while the other decided to invest in Vicodin and heroin. Different choices. So, when you hear people in government talk about wanting to make all things equal for people, how can you make these two men equal? They are different men with different choices. The same man isn't even equal to himself on different days. I'm a better person today than I was yesterday.

One million dollars is not a lot of money. Anything you think is unattainable, you'll never attain. Something that appears big and unattainable has to become small to you to be within reach.

We had to have that mentality about crusades. If you had told me when I was 24 years old that 9,000 people were coming to a meeting in America to hear me preach, I would have believed the Lord could do that but thought it would involve angels bringing people at sword point. Once I began learning how to do things, what used to be unattainable became attainable. I know that sounds wild, but that's how it works.

"Jonathan said a million dollars isn't a lot of money." A million dollars is not a lot of money. I know people disagree with me, but I'm right. Any economist will tell you I'm right, not Christians or prosperity preachers.

On the game show "Deal or No Deal," they'll ask somebody who's going to win $400,000, "What are you going to do when you win the money?"

"I'm going to buy a house for myself, and I'm going to buy a boat for my parents. And my kids are starting college, so I'm going to put them through college." No, you're not—not with that money. Your $400,000 will very quickly become about $260,000 after taxes. Maybe you could buy a house depending on what part of the country you live in, but that will only cover half the cost of a house in many places. So, what do you desire that doesn't require millions of dollars? Nothing.

You can obviously go after a dream that is less than a million. Everyone starts that way, but you're not going to have any regional, national, or worldwide dream for under a million dollars.

You must realize that a million dollars is not a lot of money. A million dollars is attainable. A million is like an entry point. I'm glad the Lord taught me this, so when someone gave our ministry one million dollars, I didn't light up and start buying luxury cars or anything else. Instead, I realized that it would run out if I didn't sow a large portion of it.

Wherever you are right now, I want you to say, "One million dollars is attainable for me." It is attainable. Go after a big thing and tell yourself it's a small thing. Just look at it like it's no big deal. Never allow Goliath to be big in your eyes. Goliath was big in the eyes of the Israelite soldiers, so they wouldn't fight him, but to David he was small. To David, he was just another lion or bear that the Lord would deliver into his hand.

"$1 million is attainable for me. It's not a lot of money." Once you understand that, you can start moving into bigger things. The day will come when the Lord expands your dream and what He's given you to do, and then a million dollars won't be a benchmark. You'll surpass that and require more.

If somebody sent a million-dollar check into our ministry right now, I would be very thankful. However, it wouldn't change one thing we're doing. That's because our ministry requires a million dollars about every 10 weeks to break even. One million dollars will last me 10 weeks, so it's not something that will make us go out and party. I began to see it as small in my mind and in my faith, and it became small. Don't treat it like a giant. Treat it as something attainable like David did Goliath.

If we were doing this teaching in the early 1900s, I wouldn't say this. I wouldn't say a million dollars isn't a big deal because in 1910 a million dollars was a very big deal. You could have bought a property in the financial district in Manhattan for less than a million dollars. But not now. So, I'm not saying it like some kind of rich jackass; I'm saying it realistically because of inflation.

There was a guy I knew in a foreign country, a third-world country. I met him when I was doing ministry in that country, and later, he messaged me. He was a businessman, and he was going to kill himself because he was in debt, and he couldn't pay it. That debt was crushing him, and he was not joking around. So, I said, "How much do you owe?" And he told me, in his currency, it was a lot. But in American currency, it was about $7,000. So, I asked him for the address to his nearest Western Union, and I wired him the $7,000. This was a long time ago, probably in 2011. He had come out of a religion that believed in reincarnation, and it's common for people in these circumstances to kill themselves, especially if they believe they're going to come back anyway. So, I wired him the $7,000. He profusely thanked me.

When we got off the phone, I laughed and thought, "That is insane that somebody was going to kill themselves over $7,000." I can't believe somebody would worry about such a small amount of money.

When I thought that, I felt the Lord speak to me in my spirit, "That's exactly how I feel when you worry about money." I thought, "Man, that's a lot for him. But for me, it isn't. Certainly not worth your life." And God said, "And I'm in heaven. Any amount of money you require pertaining to life and godliness I have under the cushions of my couch up here in heaven. I paved the streets with gold. I have priceless stones as decorations." So, you have to think about money, like God thinks about money.

ONE MILLION DOLLARS IS A REQUIREMENT TO LIVE THE CHRISTIAN LIFE

A million dollars is a requirement to live the Christian life. This is one of those statements somebody might criticize and say, "Jonathan teaches that you need a million dollars just to be a Christian." You do. I'll give you two Scriptures, and I can give you a lot more.

> A good man leaves an inheritance to his children's children...
>
> — PROVERBS 13:22 (NKJV)

If you're going to leave an inheritance to your children, you will need to come into millions of dollars. If you're going to leave an inheritance that when your children get done using it, there's still money left for your grandchildren. You're talking about many millions of dollars. "Well, I don't think that is what it means. Jonathan, it doesn't say leaves money to them. It says an inheritance. It could be a spiritual inheritance." Yeah, that too. But if you're going to read the Bible in context, did Abraham only leave spiritual things to Isaac and Jacob, or did Abraham, as a righteous man, leave wealth that Isaac and Jacob were still enjoying? Wells, land, cattle. Don't become blind to that part of the Bible. Abraham left land and cattle to his son and his grandchildren. So how was he able to do that? By the blessing of the Lord. Do we have that same blessing, or do we have a lesser blessing? The Bible says in Galatians 3: *The same blessing that God promised Abraham belongs to you.*

It's insane that any person who turns 20 and 21 has to look for an apartment. That's how you know the generations before you were delinquent in their Bible responsibilities. Orthodox Jews don't do that. Hasidic Jews don't do that. They gift their family property and usually a gift to make money. Now, obviously, you can't make a generalized statement. There are poor people of every ethnicity, but very few among Orthodox and Hasidic Jews, because they do what the Bible says. They shoot for the correct target. They understand that their life is not only supposed to be just for them and their wife to enjoy life; they also understand the need to create and lay up wealth for their children's children. My daughter's children should be impacted by my overflowing cup.

> "Then the King will say to those on his right, 'Come, you who are blessed by my father, inherit the Kingdom prepared for you from the creation of the world. For I was hungry, and you fed me. I was thirsty, and you gave me a drink. I was a stranger, and you invited me into your home. I was naked, and you gave me clothing. I was sick, and you cared for me. I was in prison, and you visited me.'
> "Then these righteous ones will reply, 'Lord, when did we ever see you hungry and feed you? Or thirsty and give you something to drink? Or a stranger and show you hospitality? Or naked and give you

> clothing? When did we ever see you sick or in prison and visit you?'
>
> "And the King will say, 'I tell you the truth, when you did it to one of the least of these my brothers and sisters, you were doing it to me!'
>
> "Then the King will turn to those on the left and say, 'Away with you, you cursed ones, into the eternal fire prepared for the devil and his demons. For I was hungry, and you didn't feed me. I was thirsty, and you didn't give me a drink. I was a stranger, and you didn't invite me into your home. I was naked, and you didn't give me clothing. I was sick and in prison, and you didn't visit me.'
>
> "Then they will reply, 'Lord, when did we ever see you hungry or thirsty or a stranger or naked or sick or in prison, and not help you?'
>
> "And he'll answer, 'I tell you the truth, when you refused to help the least of these my brothers and sisters, you were refusing to help me.'"
>
> — MATTHEW 25:34-45

I take that Scripture literally. That was my entire motivation for preaching in prison. I don't feel any call to preach in prison; I didn't feel any burden to preach to people in prison, but if Jesus said that there's going to be a group of people that when ignored, He says: *I was in prison, and you never visited me,* then I want to make sure to check that off the list. So, if you're going to take the Bible literally, which you should, the Christian is required not just to feed their family. They are called to feed people who are hungry and don't have food, clothe people who don't have clothes, and give people something to drink who are lacking.

How much money would you say all the above requires? It requires quite a bit of money just to take care of your own family, does it not? So, if you're going to have an overflow, where you start taking care of other people's children, how much will that require you to have? Now, just add in the Scripture that says a righteous man leaves an inheritance to his children's children, you're probably already into the $10 to $15 million range—true or false? Millions are required to live the true Christian life, let alone accomplish your dreams.

It's required. It won't be like something you chuckle about if you see it as a requirement. What did Jesus say? The blind shall see, the deaf hear, the cripple walk. The lepers are cleansed. The poor are given money? No, the poor are having the gospel preached to them. The cure for poverty, the thing that produces career and financial breakthrough, is the Word understood and applied to a person's life. But everybody would rather just have prayer. The Word works. In Matthew 7:24-27, you'll see that the man who builds his life and his teaching on the Word is like a wise man that builds his house on a rock. The winds blow, and the waves crash, but the house still stands firm. Building your life on the principles of God's Word is what brings true and lasting change to your economic reality. Knowing the Word will cause you to prevail.

DEVELOP A WRITTEN ACTION PLAN FOR A MILLION DOLLARS

Develop a written action plan that becomes your path to a million dollars. Consider the lady's comment on my uncle's tweet, "I don't think any pastor should have a million dollars." Let's take all the supernatural elements away. Take out, all sowing and reaping. Let's just do some math. A pastor makes $60,000 a year, and his wife makes $40,000 a year, working outside of the church, and they save

10% of that every year. That comes to $10,000 a year they save, and they put it in an investment account that earns 7% annual interest. Will they become multi-millionaires by the time they are 65, if not before? With proper financial management, it will be easy to become a multi-millionaire. Do you see that? That's why I want to sit down with the dumb lady who tweeted that no pastor should be a millionaire and say, "So if someone saves 10% of an average salary, a husband and wife, invested at 7%, explain why they should not become millionaires?"

I'm talking a million with an M. Now, I agree if somebody wanted to say a billion dollars is a lot of money. If somebody wanted to say, "I don't think I can become a billionaire," I understand why you feel that way. One thing that really irritates me is when you start teaching about millions, there's always some charismatic Christian that claims, "I'm believing for billions." Well, congratulations. But right now, you've got about $300, so let's start small. "I'm believing for trillions." Okay. Congratulations. But before you get to a billion and before you get to a trillion, you must cross a million. So, let's talk about that.

There was a preacher who lost his church and is out of the ministry, but he had a decent-sized church. When Brother R.W. Schambach told people how to fill out a check to his ministry, he'd say, "You spell thousand, T-H-O-U-S-A-N-D," to get people thinking bigger. Well, this preacher had heard Brother Schambach say that, so he said, "If you're making out a check to our church, make it out to…" and they would say the name of the church, "And you spell billions, B-I-L-L-I-O-N-S." First of all, you never write billions on a check. I'm giving you, "$4 billion dollars." It is a billion. And then secondly, if you have a billion dollars in your checking account, you're kind of a moron.

It's like there are just two ends of Christianity. You have the "No one can ever have a million," and then you have the "I'm believing to take over nations." You have Christians who say, "Some people are going soul-winning, but God didn't say make disciples. He said to make disciples of nations. I'm going to take nations, bro." No, I don't think you are, to be honest. I've met you; I've been around you. You will do well to pay your car insurance. I mean it, and I'm not just joking around or sarcastic because I hate anti-prosperity just as much as I hate pie-in-the-sky prosperity.

You might build mansions, but you're two rent payments behind right now, so let's talk practical things. Develop a written, actionable path to a million. I gave an example of the actionable path with the 25-year-old pastor and his wife, who started saving $10,000 a year at 7% interest. I just told you how someone on an average salary, not saving an insane amount of money, could die with multiple millions in their account. That's not a small amount of money. Now, if you give them another 20 years, they die, and they leave that in an account for their grandchildren that their grandchildren can't touch for another 20 years. They've trained their children enough that their children don't need the money because they're already doing well, they're doing what the Bible says.

You don't have to start a company like Walmart to change things for your family. I want to get you thinking differently. I had a revelation one time, not from the Word, but when I first started in evangelism. My goal was to book a full schedule. As I approached two years of praying and believing God for a full preaching schedule, my father said something that messed me up. He said, "Think of this... If you preach 50 Sundays a year and average $1,000 every Sunday, the most you can ever make a year is $50,000."

I thought, "Oh, so my goal of having a full schedule will never bring me a supply that enables me to reach the world. So, I'm shooting for the wrong thing. It can never happen the way I'm doing it." Well then, so how could it happen?

Start looking at the Bible, and in Luke 8:1-3 Jesus had women who traveled with Him that the Bible says regularly supported from their own resources, for Jesus to travel and preach the gospel. Elisha had the same thing with a Shunammite woman. Paul had the same thing with the Philippian church. That's where you get the Bible concept of ministry partnership. At the time, I had two partners. So, I thought, "Well, I would probably require a minimum of a million dollars in revenue a year to do the things I'd like to do in the ministry—be on television and do crusades."

This is what I'm talking about when I say a written actionable path to a million. "I have two partners right now who believe in my ministry and give every month. How many would I need to reach so that a million a year is coming in? Well, what's a million divided by 12... 8,400. So, I need 1000 partners averaging $84 a month. And that will produce $1 million of revenue, which will give me the start of doing what God is calling me to do."

My goal seemed completely unattainable, but you know what I did? The first magazine we ever made; it said Revival Today Air Force. I called it Air Force because it was to help me go on television. We were buying affiliate time on Fox and ABC. I said, "If you'd like to be a part of Revival Today Air Force, I'm believing God for 1,000 people who will give $84 a month to make that possible." It took about five years of putting that vision out there. Today, we have far surpassed that. That partnership concept was a game-changer. And it all started with me pursuing the path to find the revenue instead of thinking, "Oh, a million dollars, that'd be nice." If you have a target that seems unattainable, you have to see that it's attainable and then begin to use your brain to develop a path to that place. When you start using your brain, the Lord will get behind you and give you ideas to help you.

If the person with seven million has one 10th of the anointing as the person with $70, they could reach 100,000 times more souls. We will go on Daystar Television and preach for one hour in a few weeks. It costs a lot of money, but not as much money as traveling and preaching to the large volumes of people in different areas where Daystar is broadcasting. So, if you're a truck driver making $67,000 a year, start a sixth-day project. You work five days a week, and one day belongs to the Lord. That sixth day, get something off the ground that you control. See what happens. Give God a vessel for Him to pour oil into.

Now here's an interesting thing about a message like this. You have the same amount of money in the bank as when you started reading this, and now you might even feel like a multi-millionaire already. Now you know how to do it, and it gets exciting.

Start dreaming. I'm telling you, you can do it. You don't have to hustle or be slimy. It's a plan. Stay with the plan. Don't get discouraged. Don't get sidetracked. Don't quit something and start something else. Pick something, lay out a path, and stay on the path. It's amazing how much you can do in life just by being consistent and not repeatedly getting enamored by new things. Mark out your path and stay straight.

I look forward to hearing your testimonies.

LAW TWENTY

THE LAW OF CONTINUAL VICTORY AND INCREASE

From glory to glory, from strength to strength, from victory to victory, I'm calling this final law, The Law of Continual Victory and Increase. If you grasp what I'm teaching you in this chapter, it will change your life.

> They go from strength to strength, every one of them in Zion appeareth before God.
>
> — PSALM 84:7 (KJV)

> But we all, with open face beholding as in a glass the glory of the Lord, are changed into the same image from glory to glory, even as by the Spirit of the Lord.
>
> — 2 CORINTHIANS 3:18 (KJV)

And it shall come to pass, if thou shalt hearken diligently unto the voice of the LORD thy God, to observe and to do all his commandments which I command thee this day, that the LORD thy God will set thee on high above all nations of the earth:
And all these blessings shall come on thee, and overtake thee, if thou shalt hearken unto the voice of the LORD thy God.
Blessed shalt thou be in the city, and
blessed shalt thou be in the field.
Blessed shall be the fruit of thy body, and the fruit of thy ground, and the fruit of thy cattle, the increase of thy kine, and the flocks of thy sheep.
Blessed shall be thy basket and thy store.
Blessed shalt thou be when thou comest in, and blessed shalt thou be when thou goest out.
The LORD shall cause thine enemies that rise up against thee to be smitten before thy face: they shall come out against thee one way, and flee before thee seven ways.
The LORD shall command the blessing upon thee in thy storehouses, and in all that thou settest thine hand unto; and he shall bless thee in the land which the LORD thy God giveth thee.
The LORD shall establish thee an holy people unto himself, as he hath sworn unto thee, if thou shalt keep the commandments of the LORD thy God, and walk in his ways.
And all people of the earth shall see that thou art called by the name of the LORD; and they shall be afraid of thee.
And the LORD shall make thee plenteous in goods, in

> the fruit of thy body, and in the fruit of thy cattle, and in the fruit of thy ground, in the land which the LORD sware unto thy fathers to give thee.
> The LORD shall open unto thee his good treasure, the heaven to give the rain unto thy land in his season, and to bless all the work of thine hand: and thou shalt lend unto many nations, and thou shalt not borrow. And the LORD shall make thee the head, and not the tail; and thou shalt be above only, and thou shalt not be beneath; if that thou hearken unto the commandments of the LORD thy God, which I command thee this day, to observe and to do them:
> And thou shalt not go aside from any of the words which I command thee this day, to the right hand, or to the left, to go after other gods to serve them.
>
> — DEUTERONOMY 28:1-14 (KJV)

I can't speak for you, but I can speak for me. I've been to many churches, and I've heard preachers teach this overarching theology of mountains and valleys. They say, "Sometimes you're up, sometimes you're down. The God of the mountain is the God of the valley. Sometimes things are going good; sometimes things are going bad." And then you hear people, even though it's not in Scripture, just run with the analogy as if it was in the Scripture. They'll say, "Well, how many of you know that you can't go from one mountain top to another mountain top without going through a valley?" Well, that's true, but this is not geography class. This is the Bible, and the Bible does not teach a life of mountains and valleys.

As a teenager, I remember summer camp being a powerful week with God. In that week, the presence of the Lord was thick in the services;

I was profoundly touched by God. Upon our return to church on Sunday, everybody was singing at the top of their lungs; all the youth during praise and worship had hands lifted, worshiping God. Then, our pastor gets up and says, "Isn't it great to see our young people so on fire for God? You went out to camp and had a mountaintop experience. But how many of you know you can't stay on the mountaintop? You have to go into the valley."

At that time, I hadn't received any teaching along the lines of what I'm teaching you today, but the pastor's words didn't hit my spirit right. At 16-years-old, I thought, "No, I don't think God did everything He did this last week so I could go back to where I was. I believe God took me somewhere in the spirit and His plan for me is to keep advancing." The truth came out later that the pastor who said this was having an affair with one of the ladies in the choir. It turns out, according to the Bible, I wasn't wrong.

They go from glory to glory, not glory to shame, then back to glory. They go from glory to glory. Those who appear before the Lord on Mount Zion, go from strength to strength, not from strength to weakness to strength. From glory to glory, from strength to strength.

Deuteronomy 28 says *if your enemy attacks you from one direction, he'll flee from you in seven. You will always be the head. You will never be the tail. You will always be on top. You'll never be at the bottom.* How do you get mountains and valleys out of this?

The Bible specifically says *as long as you hearken to do what I've said in my Word, and don't run after other gods and serve them, I'll put you always on top. Always on top and never at the bottom.* You'll never know what bottom is; you'll never know what it means to be the tail. The tail is a thing that's so useless, God didn't even give man one. They don't even know what its function is on a dog. You'll always be the head. How many times? Always. Glory to glory, victory to victory, and strength to strength. The law of continual victory and increase—from glory to glory.

The Bible does not teach a doctrine of mountains and valleys. Whatever you believe, you become. The Devil wants it to become the pervasive thought of Christians that life is full of ups and downs. I'm telling you right now, you could go to about any charismatic or full-gospel church and say from the platform, "How many of you know that life is full of ups and downs," and all the hands would go up.

Is it any wonder why the average church member is faithful to church two or three weeks, then goes missing for a month and a half? It was preached to them. They were told that life's made of spiritual ups and downs. That's what my pastor told me growing up—spiritually, I would have a great experience with God, then I would have to come back down to where I was. But the Bible, thankfully, doesn't teach that. From glory to glory, victory to victory, and strength to strength, that's what the Bible says.

At the time of this writing, I saw a Christian leader tweet, "Every Christian is a struggling Christian." The tweet had 2,000 likes and over 200 re-tweets. So, I re-tweeted it and wrote, "Oh? I'd like that explained to me." I can tell you that I'm not saying this just to be positive; I am not struggling. This ministry is not struggling. My marriage isn't struggling. My child's not struggling. It never will because it's unscriptural for a Christian to be struggling, or to be in a position of struggling. Do storms come? Yes. Can storms affect the trajectory of the boat that has Christ in it? No. God gave us too many weapons to ever allow a storm to sink our boat, stall our boat, or make our boat turn back. The kingdom of God is not built on struggling. The kingdom of God is built on increase.

It is impossible to follow after God's Word and decrease. You won't find anybody in the Bible that was rich when they gave their life to

God and poor when they finished. But you will find the opposite; many nobodies began to give themselves to God and go higher.

I'm not saying it's impossible to be a Christian and decrease. Being a Christian is like meeting people wearing Pittsburgh Steelers jerseys and thinking they're all part of the team. But, if they try to go on the field, security will put them in prison. They have the jersey, know all the coaches, know all the players, and know everything about the Steelers, but they're not a Steeler. There are a lot of Christians that have the uniform. They have the book, but the Bible didn't say, "If you decide to become a follower of me, then all these things will happen." It says: *If you diligently hearken to do all the things I've commanded you to do.*

What does it mean to diligently hearken unto what God's Word is saying? It's not listening; it's diligently hearkening. What's the difference between diligent hearkening and just listening?

When I took a biology class in high school, I listened to what the teacher said. When I took a skydiving class so I could skydive without the instructor, I diligently hearkened. I asked questions. They didn't have to say, "Does anybody have any questions?" Instead, I asked, "Excuse me, go over that last part again. Excuse me, you said if the chute doesn't open, the backup chute cord is where? Excuse me, I have to wait until I've dropped at least how many thousand feet before I open the chute to avoid getting tangled in the aircraft?" It mattered to me. Biology did not matter to me. I did just enough to pass the test so I wouldn't be held back. But when my life was on the line, I wanted to know everything I needed to do. That's diligent hearkening.

I feel the same way about the Bible because my life is on the line. This is the difference between divorce and successful marriage. It's the difference between having children that fall away from God or children that carry the torch. It's the difference between financial stress and financial abundance, which is a universe of difference. What a difference. It's the difference between long life and health and early death and sickness.

The Bible says: *He that departs from the path of understanding shall abide in the congregation of the dead.* Therefore, anything in the Bible you don't understand, if you act on that misunderstanding, you abide in the congregation of the dead. According to Scripture, you live a life no different from someone who's spiritually dead.

Regarding the Christian leader who wrote, "Every Christian is a struggling Christian," what do you think he would say if I brought these things up to him? I'll tell you what he'd say… He'd say one of two things: "I don't know, I never knew that," or, "I don't believe that." Whatever you don't believe won't work for you.

The only way the Word works for you is by faith, and faith is full-heart belief in what God said. Abraham believed those things spoken to him, and God counted it as righteousness unto him. How would you defend the statement that every Christian is a struggling Christian in light of the Scriptures we read above? How do you read Deuteronomy 28:1-14 and say every Christian is a struggling Christian? How do you read Joshua 1 and state that every Christian is a struggling Christian?

> "Moses my servant is dead. Therefore, the time has come for you to lead these people, the Israelites, across the Jordan River into the land I am giving them. I promise you what I promised Moses: 'Wherever you set foot, you will be on land I have given you— from the Negev wilderness in the south to the Lebanon mountains in the north, from

> the Euphrates River in the east to the Mediterranean Sea in the west, including all the land of the Hittites.' No one will be able to stand against you as long as you live. For I will be with you as I was with Moses. I will not fail you or abandon you.
>
> "Be strong and courageous, for you are the one who will lead these people to possess all the land I swore to their ancestors I would give them. Be strong and very courageous. Be careful to obey all the instructions Moses gave you. Do not deviate from them, turning either to the right or to the left. Then you will be successful in everything you do."
>
> — JOSHUA 1:2-7

I don't understand how you read that and say every Christian is a struggling Christian. It does not say you will struggle in everything you do. In fact, it says the exact opposite. You will be successful in everything you do.

If you stay in the book of Joshua, go to chapter 7 and see that they are undefeated for six chapters. Then in chapter 7, they get defeated by a town called Ai. When they lost that battle, Joshua threw himself on the ground and began to cry out to God and ask what the problem was. If Joshua was a believer who thought all believers are struggling believers, then he would have lost that battle and said, "Well, it's about time. We've been winning battles for six chapters straight. Only a matter of time, you can't win them all." But actually, when they suffered defeat, there was such a revulsion in him against defeat that he knew it was unscriptural.

Understand that if you receive the other doctrine, you don't have any resistance in you when things go wrong. "Doctor said, my eyesight's failing. I am in my fifties now." Well, miracles start when you get disgusted with something that's happening. So, if you think poverty is normal, you're never going to operate in supernatural wealth. If you think sickness is normal, you're never going to attain divine healing. If you think a broken home is normal, your marriage will be full of struggle.

Everything begins with the understanding that the believer has been granted good success. So, if something's not working, there's a problem. You need to find out what it is and root it out.

If I'm having the worst voyage I've ever had, there's a Jonah on board. Or I am Jonah, and I need to throw myself overboard and go in the direction God called me to. Something's wrong, and I need to take care of it. If it's a demon, I have authority over demons, so that's nothing to blame. The Devil's not over your head. The Devil is under your feet permanently.

There's a quote I love that says, "No man is a failure until he starts looking for who to blame." Blaming will keep you in failure. Blaming the Devil, blaming generational curses, blaming demons, blaming racism, blaming any outside person, force, or factor when the Bible tells you that if you do what God tells you to do, you will have good success. I will bless all the work of your hands. You will become plenteous in goods.

The kingdom of God is not built on struggling. The kingdom of God is built on increase. If I was going to post a tweet, I wouldn't write, "Every Christian is a struggling Christian." I would write, "Every Christian is an overcoming Christian. Every Christian is a victorious Christian."

> To him who overcomes I will grant to sit with Me on
> My throne, as I also overcame and sat down with
> My Father on His throne.
>
> — REVELATION 3:21 (NKJV)

Heaven is the home of overcomers. It doesn't say to all who struggle, who've struggled, I'll cause them to sit down on my throne. It says to him who overcomes. Overcoming is the opposite of struggling. Struggling is negative, defeat is negative. Is it not abundance that Christ promised? When you're in victory, the air smells sweeter. You enjoy being around people. Heaven is not the home of strugglers. Heaven is the home of those who overcome.

> For if these things be in you, and abound, they
> make you that ye shall neither be barren nor
> unfruitful in the knowledge of our Lord Jesus
> Christ.
> But he that lacketh these things is blind, and cannot see
> afar off, and hath forgotten that he was purged
> from his old sins.
> Wherefore the rather, brethren, give diligence to make
> your calling and election sure: for if ye do these
> things, ye shall never fall:
> For so an entrance shall be ministered unto you
> abundantly into the everlasting kingdom of our
> Lord and Saviour Jesus Christ.
>
> — 2 PETER 1:8-11 (KJV)

The Christian life is an overcoming life. The Christian life is a victorious life. The Christian life is the ever-increasing life. The

Christian life is the good success life. The Christian life is the abundant life. Jesus said I have come that you might have life and have it more abundantly; that's the Christian life. You don't get struggling out of that.

The Christian life is not only an overcoming life, it is a continually overcoming life. From glory to glory, victory to victory, and strength to strength. Higher heights. You'll never reach the top level in God. When God told Solomon, "I'm going to make you rich," he was already rich. You will never hit the top level with God. Continually overcoming, ever-increasing.

> Oh, the joys of those who do not
> follow the advice of the wicked,
> or stand around with sinners,
> or join in with mockers.
> But they delight in the law of the LORD,
> meditating on it day and night.
> They are like trees planted along the riverbank,
> bearing fruit each season.
> Their leaves never wither,
> and they prosper in all they do.
>
> — PSALM 1:1-3

If you say things like, "We're going through kind of a dry season right now. This hasn't really been a season of growth for our ministry or our business," you have bad doctrine, and anytime you invite bad doctrine, the Devil will help accommodate it.

I want you to confess this: "In every season, I bear fruit." You can be a fruitful child. You can be a fruitful teenager. You can be a fruitful young adult. You can be fruitful in your forties. You can be fruitful when your friends are winding down. At 55, you can be bearing the most fruit you've ever borne. You can be a fruitful senior, like Moses was. There's no age where there's not an anointing to be fruitful. There's no season of fruitlessness for the Christian. It doesn't matter who the president is. Doesn't matter what laws are being passed. The harsher the laws passed against the Israelites in Egypt, the more they multiplied. No external force can hinder the supernatural law that God's made available to you. In every season, I bear fruit.

Every occupation allows a time of fruitlessness. If you talk to people who sell cars, there are certain months when people don't buy cars. If you talk to realtors, there are certain months when people don't buy as many homes. If you talk to evangelists, there are months when it's hard to get meetings. If you talk to pastors, there are months when people go away, and church attendance is down. So, people subconsciously have allotted themselves times of fruitlessness. They expect lack during certain times of the year. Whatever you expect, is what you'll experience. The expectation of the righteous will not be cut off.

I heard Bishop David Oyedepo teach on this. From the day I heard him teach on it and received what he had to say, it has been astounding what's taken place in our lives and ministry. I heard him say that if this is true, and it is, every month should increase from the month before. I thought, "Man, I don't know if that's possible." Let alone every year, increase on the year before. Every month should increase more than the month before?

I see it in the Bible, continual increase. From strength to strength, and from glory to glory. Next month should be more glorious than this month. This month should be more glorious than last month. I started to set my faith and my confession in that direction.

I got last month's financial report for our ministry. We took in double the amount of money last month than we had years ago for the entire year! The year I received this revelation, we quadrupled the ministry's revenue from the year before, then doubled it the next year. And I thought, well, surely you can't keep doubling every year. But it just keeps going. During the pandemic, we increased more. The external factors don't matter. By believing the Word of God, receiving the Word of God, speaking it, and acting on it, you tap into an uncancellable law, the law of continual victory and increase.

AFTERWORD

If someone does not care about money, they do not care about people, their own life, their family, or their own dreams and accomplishments, and they have little or no regard for the Gospel of Jesus Christ.

By understanding the laws governing the financial anointing and attracting wealth into one's life, money becomes a means of living a productive life and making a positive impact on this world and the world to come. It's about fulfilling the calling God has placed upon your life

The Bible speaks of a financial anointing that negates the need for fundraising, while supernaturally attracting wealth. There is a supernatural anointing that affects money and provision. Just as laws govern science, thermodynamics, and health, there are laws governing the financial anointing. We've just explored 20 of them together.

AFTERWORD

1. The Law of Positive Outlook

2. The Elisha Law: Looking to Pay

3. The Law of Contentment

4. The Law of Proper Value

5. The Law of Servanthood

6. The Law of Solution

7. The Law of Association

8. The Law of Covenant Land Ownership

9. The Law of The Family

10. The Law of Joy

11. The Law of Protection

12. The Law of Debt Refusal

13. The Law of Holiness

14. The Law of Love and Honor

15. The Law of Significant Seed Sowing

16. The Law of Diligence

17. The Law of Confession

18. The Law of Thanksgiving and Praise

19. The Millionaire Law

20. The Law of Continual Victory and Increase

AFTERWORD

God has commanded you to increase. Religion has a problem with you thinking that way, but God has a problem with you not looking to increase.

Get your thinking straight on this and receive the financial anointing. The last defeat you saw will be the last defeat you ever see. The last backward step you took will be the last backward step you ever take. No more ups and downs, just ups and ups. From glory to glory, victory to victory, and strength to strength. That's what God has allotted for you, and you should make up your mind that you're going to begin walking that way today. "This will be the best month I've ever had, and next month will improve upon this month."

No more dry seasons. Whatever job you're in, don't repeat what heathen people say. "Well, in the winter we don't sell many cars." Well, if you don't, it's because of your own confession. When men say there's a casting down, you will say, there's a lifting up. Try it sometime where you work. When they say this winter is not looking good. Say, "I'm going to have the best winter I've ever had." Say stuff like that aloud, and watch God confirm it because He loves when somebody believes and speaks His Word.

What you confess (agree with) matters. You may be reading this book, and if you're honest with yourself, you can't point to a time when you ever prayed the prayer of salvation. You need to confess Jesus as Lord of your life, repent from sin, and turn toward Him; He'll set you free! You can do this yourself anywhere and anytime but it's also important to tell someone. The Revival Today Staff is available to pray with you and to celebrate your confession. Call 412-787-2578 to talk to a real person who cares about you, and who will pray with you and for you. It's the most important decision you will ever make!

"My generation shall be saved!"

— JONATHAN SHUTTLESWORTH

ABOUT THE AUTHOR

Evangelist and Pastor, Jonathan Shuttlesworth, is the founder of Revival Today and Pastor of Revival Today Church, ministries dedicated to reaching lost and hurting people with The Gospel of Jesus Christ.

In fulfilling his calling, Jonathan Shuttlesworth has conducted meetings and open-air crusades throughout North America, India, the Caribbean, and Central and South Africa.

Revival Today Church was launched in 2022 as a soul-winning, Holy Spirit honoring church that is unapologetic about believing the Bible to bless families and nations.

Each day thousands of lives are impacted globally through Revival Today Broadcasting and Revival Today Church, located in Pittsburgh, Pennsylvania.

While methods may change, Revival Today's heartbeat remains for the lost, providing biblical teaching on faith, healing, prosperity, freedom from sin, and living a victorious life.

If you need help or would like to partner with Revival Today to see this generation and nation transformed through The Gospel, follow these links…

Contact Revival Today

www.RevivalToday.com
www.RevivalTodayChurch.com

Get access to our 24/7 network Revival Today Global Broadcast. Download the Revival Today app in your Apple App Store or Google Play Store. Watch live on Apple TV, Roku, Amazon Fire TV, and Android TV.

Call: 412-787-2578

- facebook.com/revivaltoday
- twitter.com/jdshuttlesworth
- instagram.com/jdshuttlesworth
- youtube.com/@jonathanshuttlesworth

www.ingramcontent.com/pod-product-compliance
Lightning Source LLC
Chambersburg PA
CBHW021146160426
43194CB00007B/710